A Short History of Lake Tahoe

A SHORT HISTORY OF

Lake Tahoe

MICHAEL J. MAKLEY

WITHDRAWN

UNIVERSITY OF NEVADA PRESS RENO & LAS VEGAS

University of Nevada Press, Reno, Nevada 89557 USA
Copyright © 2011 by University of Nevada Press
All rights reserved
Manufactured in the United States of America
Design by Kathleen Szawiola

Library of Congress Cataloging-in-Publication Data

Makley, Michael J.
A short history of Lake Tahoe / Michael J. Makley.
   p.   cm.
Includes bibliographical references and index.
ISBN 978-0-87417-850-0 (pbk. : alk. paper)
1. Tahoe, Lake (Calif. and Nev.)—History. 2. Natural history—Tahoe, Lake
(Calif. and Nev.) 3. Tahoe, Lake (Calif. and Nev.)—Environmental conditions.
4. Tahoe, Lake, Region (Calif. and Nev.)—History. 5. Tahoe, Lake, Region
(Calif. and Nev.)—Biography. I. Title.
F868.T2M35 2011
979.4'38—dc22   2011013725

FIRST PRINTING
20   19   18   17   16   15   14   13   12   11
5   4   3   2   1

Frontispiece: Lake Tahoe from Cave Rock in the nineteenth century.
(Courtesy Special Collections, University of Nevada, Reno Library.)

For my brother, Kevin, and Stephen Ledyard
with whom I shared a magical time
growing up at Tahoe

Contents

Preface

People come to Lake Tahoe for many reasons. From its ten-thousand-foot peaks to its pine forests and sandy beaches, there is magic in this region. Temperatures are moderate in summer, and its winters produce beautiful snow-covered landscapes. Tourist attractions and outdoor recreation possibilities in all seasons are extraordinary. The area hosts the largest concentration of ski areas in North America while averaging more than three hundred sunny days a year. Yet its human and environmental histories are not widely known.

The lake is the center of Washoe Indian lands, and the tribe has an extensive mythology and oral history regarding its environs. Washoes see themselves as caretakers of the area's animals, land, water, and air. Over the course of many hundreds of years, they lived at the lake from spring until fall, and the natural environment prospered.

The relatively brief European American history at Tahoe begins in the middle of the nineteenth century. Awestruck by its beauty, arriving Americans nevertheless were intent on "conquering the wilderness." They were acquisitive with an eye toward harvesting its abundant resources for use in distant vistas. Within a half century, the lake basin's forests and fisheries were destroyed, the water's remarkable clarity dramatically reduced.

Regenerated by the second half of the twentieth century, Tahoe's beauty led to ever-increasing numbers of residents and visitors and incessant building. Air quality and water clarity again suffered devastating effects. Disputes over the amount of human activity that should be allowed and to what degree conservation was needed continued into the twenty-first century. Scientific studies and political infighting eventually led to compromises involving residents, businesspeople, ecologists, and local and regional agencies. The cooperative efforts allowed protections to be put in place that today provide encouraging signs of another environmental revival.

This narrative describes the events, forces, and factors that have affected the course of developments in the lake basin while portraying the visionaries, schemers, and eccentrics who influenced them. In the end, the lake's history can be seen as a cautionary ecological tale as well as a fascinating story.

The concept of this book was proposed by Matt "Becks" Becker, University of Nevada Press editor. He has provided assistance and guidance in all its phases, steering the manuscript through the jury and editorial processes, and has earned my unreserved gratitude. Others who have lent invaluable help include former Nevada state archivist Guy Rocha; Nevada historian Robert Stewart; Laurel Ames, the first executive director of the Sierra Nevada Alliance; South Tahoe Public Utility District information officer Dennis Cocking; the late Dennis Oliver, Tahoe Regional Planning Agency; Bill Watson, manager of the Thunderbird Lodge Preservation Society; Alison Moore, California Historical Society l-ibrarian; and Darrel Bender and Art George Jr. of the Washoe Tribe. Assistance procuring photographs came from Donnelyn Curtis and Joel Guldner at the University of Nevada Special Collections; Bud Fawcett of Fawcett Photo Design; Amanda Royal and Cozette Alojzya Savage of the League to Save Lake Tahoe; Doug Haney and Katie Perhai of the U.S. Ski and Snowboard Association; Tom Milham, Lake Tahoe Wildlife Care; Tim Parsons, *Tahoe Daily Tribune;* Carole Morgan; and Jim Plehn. Line editor Annette Wenda's comprehensive knowledge and attention to detail enabled her to delete, add, and correct things that clarified and enhanced the text. I am indebted as well to University of Nevada Press director Joanne O'Hare, managing editor Sara Vélez Mallea, design manager Kathleen Szawiola, and marketing manager Barbara Berlin. I also wish to thank my mother, Dorothy Makley, who, based on her long Lake Tahoe residency, offered possibilities and sources for my research, and, as with each of my projects, Matthew Makley, who is an indispensable consultant. Finally, I owe a special debt to my wife, Randi Makley, for her steadfast support and boundless enthusiasm.

A Short History of Lake Tahoe

Introduction

Samuel Clemens sojourned at Lake Tahoe in 1861, two years before he would adopt his nom de plume, Mark Twain. In letters to his mother and sister, among other tributes, he called the lake "the masterpiece of the Creation," and concluded, "I had better stop about 'the lake,' though—for whenever I think of it I want to go there and *die,* the place is so beautiful."

In *Roughing It,* using the name Mark Twain, he described seeing the lake from a mountain pass: "We had heard a world of talk about the marvelous beauty of Lake Tahoe, and finally curiosity drove us thither to see it. . . . As it lay there with the shadows of the mountains brilliantly photographed upon its still surface I thought it must surely be the fairest picture the whole earth affords." He went on to extol the virtues of camping at the lake: "Three months of camp life on Lake Tahoe would restore an Egyptian mummy to his pristine vigor, and give him an appetite like an alligator. I do not mean the oldest and driest mummies, of course, but the fresher ones. The air up there in the clouds is very pure and fine, bracing and delicious. And why shouldn't it be?—it is the same the angels breathe."

Lake Tahoe sits atop the northern Sierra Nevada, 6,225 feet above sea level. It is 22 miles long, 12 miles wide, and 1,636 feet deep—the third-deepest lake in North America. Its waters are dissected by the California-Nevada state line, with approximately two-thirds of it in California. The

Millions of years of geologic evolution created Carson Valley, the Sierra Nevada block, and Lake Tahoe. (Courtesy Special Collections, University of Nevada, Reno, Library)

lake basin is encompassed by the Sierra Nevada crest line on its west and the Great Carson Spur, or Carson Range, on its east.

The lake's environs are the product of millions of years of geologic evolution. The original mountain block was reconfigured by massive faulting during the late Cretaceous period. The fracturing, uplifting, and dropping resulted in a spacious basin surrounded by spectacular peaks that form the area's double summit. There is more than 12,500 feet of difference between Freel Peak, the basin's highest mountain at 10,881 feet, and the lake's deepest point.

Over a vast period of time, the basin filled with water. Two to three million years ago, the area underwent further deformation during a period of violent volcanic action. The most prominent of the eruptions created the massive Mount Pluto in the northwest, between the lake and the Truckee River Canyon. Its lava blocked the lake's outlet, raising the water level several hundred feet higher than it is today.

A glacial epoch followed the plutonic period, and sheets of ice more than 1,000 feet deep formed. Toward the end of the last ice age, giant glaciers inched down the mountains.

Even a cursory look around the lake allows evidence of its natural history. On the east shore, Cave Rock, a volcanic plug whose spectacular jutting lines reveal the force of the lava's upward thrusts, features caves that resulted from wave action during the period of deep lake water. In the north, off Dollar Point, lava flows from Mount Pluto formed shelves now 25 feet underwater from which the lake floor drops precipitously to nearly 600 feet. Thousands of years of erosion have produced fantastic sunken cliffs, underwater canyons, amphitheaters, and valleys. On the west shore, Fallen Leaf Lake and Cascade Lake are the remnants of glaciers whose terminal moraines separate them from Tahoe. Encompassing spectacular Emerald Bay, perpendicular cliffs, many hundreds of feet high, display the glaciers' scouring effects. The cliff at the bay's head hosts Eagle Falls, a succession of three waterfalls that cascade down the sheer wall.

Up to 20 feet deep in the south shore's cold, oxygenated water, well-preserved tree stumps rise from the sediment. The stumps date as far back as 6,300 years. The well-rooted trees lived several hundred years and show to what extent the lake's level has fluctuated in the current geologic period. The cause of the reduction in depth remains in scientific dispute, most likely the result of tectonic activity or an epic drought.

Anthropologists believe the ancestral Washoe Indians arrived at Lake Tahoe 8,000 to 10,000 years ago; the Washoes disagree, believing they were created in the area. In traditional Washoe creation stories, Nentusu, the female Creator, placed them at the lake, which they called Daowaga. For hundreds of generations, Daowaga was the center of the Washoe world. During the snowless seasons of the year, they lived in homesites around its 72-mile circumference. Each of its bays, coves, inlets, beaches, and landmarks is associated with some sacred Washoe myth or secular historical event.

The arrival of Euro-Americans 160 years ago destroyed the Washoe way of life. The newcomers came in overwhelming numbers and usurped the Indians' lands. When after a few years an Indian agent recommended the Washoes be placed on a reservation, settlers said no land was available. The government did little to pursue the matter; it believed the tribe was near extinction. The Washoes were forced to adapt to the far-reaching changes.

When the Americans arrived, the lake and its sixty-three tributaries were full of silver trout and giant Tahoe cutthroat. In 1844 explorer John Frémont called the lake's only outlet, the Truckee River, Salmon Trout River because of the quantity of the subspecies of Lahontan cutthroat trout that grew to four feet long and weighed as much as forty pounds. The Washoes fished the waters in spring and summer using a wide variety of techniques, from dams, weirs, and stream diversions to plant fiber nets, spears, and four-pronged hooks—the top hooks baited with worms or fish eggs to catch minnows, the bottom one baited with a minnow to catch trout. In this last manner, bait and food were caught at the same time.

Twain wrote of spending a great deal of time fishing at Tahoe, seeing thousands of trout but rarely catching anything. He speculated that perhaps the fish could see the line too clearly in the pristine water. "We frequently selected the trout we wanted, and rested the bait patiently and persistently on the end of his nose at a depth of eighty feet, but he would only shake it off with an annoyed manner, and shift his position."

Twain's chronicle stated that although a sawmill operated three miles from their camp, "there were not fifteen other human beings throughout the wide circumference of the lake." Although this statement was an exaggeration that referred only to Americans, the surrounding Sierra and the valley were considered wilderness. The winter before, J. Ross Browne, later the U.S. commissioner of mines in Nevada and a renowned writer, walked across the mountains telling of an encounter with four large wolves, which "seemed entirely unconcerned at my presence, except in so far as they may have indulged in some speculation as to the amount of flesh contained on my body." The animals were driven off by gunfire from a teamster who happened along. The following winter a lone trapper froze to death near what later became Tahoe City.

The discovery of the Comstock Lode in nearby Virginia City, Nevada, was the impetus for the transformation of the area. Beginning in 1860 a

Lake Tahoe west from Cave Rock in the nineteenth century. (Courtesy Special Collections, University of Nevada, Reno, Library)

small army of fortune seekers proceeded to trek across the Sierra, beginning a quarter century of heavy commerce. The roads from California soon circled Lake Tahoe, and the lake basin became an important resource in Virginia City's hinterland.

Throughout the 1860s rumors about Lake Tahoe spread as if they were scientific facts. One held that the lake had no bottom, another that the water found at depth in Virginia City mines came from Tahoe, a third that diminished atmospheric pressure made the water so light that even good swimmers sank and drowned. This last rumor resulted from the fact that a number of drowning victims' bodies had never been found.

In August 1870 Joseph LeConte, the most noted geologist at the University of California, on a trek through the Sierra with a group of students, arrived at the lake. He wanted to investigate the rumor regarding the lack of water density. LeConte's students were asking for the scientific explanation, and he promised them an experiment at the right time. They rented a sailboat and sailed several miles. The professor commented on the majestic "serried peaks" close against the lake's shore "to guard its crystal purity," and the water's color, "emerald-green, and the deepest, ultramarine blue." As the day warmed, he announced it was time for the scientific experiment. He dove into the water, swam out, and floated on his back for ten minutes. The students followed, dispelling the rumor regarding atmospheric pressure and light water.

LeConte's brother, John, served as a physics professor at the university and later became one of its presidents. John LeConte visited the lake in the late summer of 1873 and made a series of soundings, experiments, and observations. The results explained the reason drowning victims' bodies did not rise. The cause was not the water's density but its temperature at great depth: in the low 40 degrees Fahrenheit below 400 feet and 39 degrees at the deepest he measured, 1,506 feet. Such cold does not allow gases usually generated by decomposition to be produced in the intestines. Once a body sinks in Tahoe, it does not inflate as it would in warmer temperatures and so does not rise. Although the lake's water mixes to its bottom every few years, the fifty-six million or so scavenging crayfish that live to 40 feet deep on the lake bed are the most likely explanation for why bodies never reappear.

In studying the transparency of the water, John LeConte used a method devised eight years earlier in the Mediterranean by the pope's scientific adviser, Angelo Secchi. He submerged a white dinner plate to different depths until it was no longer visible. In 1873 LeConte found a dish visible in Lake Tahoe to 108.27 feet.

Nearly one hundred years later, in 1968, University of California–Davis scientist Charles Goldman, whose work would gain worldwide recognition, began studying the lake. Sediment cores from the lake bottom showed that clear-cut logging in the 1870s and '80s had produced high levels of erosion and substantial loss of clarity: seven times that of its previous levels. He began regular observations, using a "Secchi dish" to record the depth of visibility. Those experiments showed that in the first half of the twentieth century, with the establishment of second-growth forests that arrested polluting silt flows into the lake, the lake's water quality had returned. Goldman's first test allowed visibility to 102 feet.

But urbanization, with its disturbances to the land, had already begun a second period of deterioration in lake clarity. Measurements after 1968 showed that pollutants were entering the water at an alarming rate. Goldman's Secchi-dish experiments revealed a loss of transparency of about a foot a year, until in the mid-1990s the level measured 60 feet. Political battles led to steps to control contaminants, and tests in the twenty-first century show translucence has risen again to near the 70-foot level: remarkable clarity if not measured against earlier times.

The record of fluctuations provides an accurate accounting of human activity at the lake. The data reinforce the narrative of social, economic, and political interaction that resulted in the use and misuse of the lake's resources. The human stories, inexorably intertwined with the fragile environment, form the history of Tahoe. The chronicle begins many centuries before the Americans' arrival, with the Washoe Indians.

Chapter One

The Washoe Indians and the Lake

*I*n the late nineteenth century the powerful Washoe shaman Welewkushkush used his powers for healing. Supernatural Water Babies, the most powerful of the Washoes' mythological beings, inhabited all rivers, lakes, streams, and ponds in the Washoe world. They were one of Welewkushkush's sources of power. Lake Tahoe, the center of the vast Washoe lands, was the center of the Water Babies' world as well. Legend held that the small, gray-skinned creatures used a tunnel running from the lake to travel to other bodies of water in the valleys of the eastern Sierra.

Once, on Tahoe's shore, Welewkushkush's apprentice collapsed, falling severely ill. Welewkushkush announced that one of the water beings had captured the apprentice's soul. He began chanting and shaking his rattle and entered the water. He proceeded until completely submerged. Witnesses, who included whites as well as Washoes, claimed the shaman remained underwater for some ten minutes. When he returned he instructed the apprentice's mother to shout the boy's name four times, and he circled the boy an equal number of times. The boy's nose began to bleed, a sign of supernatural power having touched him, and he regained consciousness. Welewkushkush turned the boy to the lake and instructed him to shake the rattle. The apprentice acted as if awakening from a dream. Welewkushkush had negotiated with the leader of the Water Babies for the boy's soul.

For thousands of years early in spring, as soon as melting snow allowed, the young and healthy Washoes traveled from their winter homes in the valleys adjoining the Sierra to the lakeshore. As the season progressed, those who took more time to travel, the elderly and perhaps mothers with babies or small children, followed. The three main branches of Washoes, the Welmelti from the North, the central Pawalti, and the Hangalelti from the South, took up residences encircling the lake for what was known as the "Big Time." Various clans spent the summer months visiting and celebrating, the elders taking time to meet and plan the use of hunting and plant resources for the following year. In the fall, Trout Creek on the south shore became one of the most important of their areas. The fish taken there were prepared and carried out as fare to be consumed while gathering pine nuts in the Great Basin or acorns on the Sierra's western slope.

With the arrival of Euro-Americans, Washoe Indians would have to adapt to far-reaching changes. (Courtesy Special Collections, University of Nevada, Reno, Library)

Upon their arrival at Daowaga, Washoes blessed the water that breathed life into their ecosystem. Throughout the summer, tribe members fished the lake and its tributaries, collected medicinal and food plants in its surrounding meadows, and, toward fall, hunted game on its mountainsides. The Upper Truckee River hosted a significant habitation site, one and a quarter miles from the lake on the river's east side. Washoes called the river *ImgiwO'tha, imgi* being cutthroat trout, *wO'tha* meaning "river." It, and the streams that fed the lake, was full of fish whose populations were maintained in various ways. Fishing leaders designated areas to be fished and would not allow unreasonable numbers to be taken. In the spring, suckers and parasitic fish were seined, and female fish were left alone. The Washoes believed the Creator had given them a sacred trust as wards of the region.

Place was of utmost importance to the Washoes. Earl James, a community leader in the 1960s, commented that the lake sustained the Washoes "as a mother, as a provider." In 2007 Art George Jr., a tribe member who follows traditional Washoe doctrine, commented, "There are many places all the way around Lake Tahoe that are very sacred to us. . . . This is a center of our spirituality, of our land's spirituality."

Cave Rock is a 360-foot monolith towering over the east shore. The massif's main cave would seem to have been an ideal homesite for early man, but the Washoes say that from time immemorial it served a different purpose. It was the shamans' sanctum: a place where they might gain or replenish their power. Other humans were forbidden to trespass there; doing so would endanger the individual, the clan, and perhaps the entire tribe. Archaeologists' findings confirm the contention. They have found no vestiges of habitation at Cave Rock. The more esoteric, or mystic, use of the site is implied by the artifacts discovered there, including the oldest objects: three basalt projectile points and an inscribed mammal bone.

In the early twentieth century historian Grace Dangberg recorded several translated Washoe tales. One called "The Weasel Brothers" describes the adventures of two mischievous weasels, Pewetseli and Damalali. The story features a scuffle between Damalali and a Water Baby that begins on the southeast shore of the lake. As they wrestle under-water, they move along the shore, and places are named: "This will be called Mortar Creek. And then they came away from there. People will call this Fish Passage. And then they came away from there. The Washoe will call this Rock Standing Gray (Cave Rock). And then they came away from there."

In another part of the weasel brothers' story, Nentusu, the Creator, counsels people who are singing, playing games, and making a great noise to be quiet. They ignore her and fall prey to a human-eating giant. Another of the mythological creatures in Washoe lore is Ang, a giant bird that nested on a rock in the lake near Cave Rock. Ang, and other monsters, preyed on humans, and through cautionary tales about them, Washoes learned to be careful and vigilant. Perhaps it is owing to the tales that when the first wave of Euro-Americans arrived in Washoe lands, the newcomers assumed the few individuals they glimpsed were neighboring Paiutes or Miwoks, not realizing a distinct tribe lived in the area.

On February 14, 1844, John C. Frémont and members of his exploration party became the first Americans to view Lake Tahoe. They were atop Red Lake Peak on Carson Pass, sixteen miles due south of the lake.

In November of that year five wagons of the eleven that composed the Elisha Stevens emigrant train became the first to cross the Sierra. The party followed the Truckee River, originally Frémont's Salmon Trout River, renamed for Chief Truckee—the Paiute Indian who guided the Stevens train. (Truckee was renowned as a leader, and his progeny included his son Chief Winnemucca, for whom the Nevada town is named, and his redoubtable granddaughter Sarah Winnemucca.) The river led to the body of water later named Donner Lake, after the tragic Donner Party that became trapped there. The Stevens group was confronted with the vast, perhaps impenetrable, mountain wall at Donner Pass. With snow on the ground and more threatening, the party split to improve their chances of survival. While the five wagons and their teams succeeded in an epic struggle to gain the pass, six members on horseback followed the Truckee to the south. They reached the river's Tahoe headwaters, becoming the first whites to set foot on the lake's shore. They skirted the northwest side of the lake to McKinney Creek, used the creek valley to gain the mountain crest, and followed tributaries of the American River to John Sutter's fort.

Some four years later John Calhoun "Cock Eye" Johnson, owner of a ranch east of Hangtown, soon renamed Placerville by self-conscious city fathers, found the great natural lake basin while searching for an alternative to the Carson Pass route established by Frémont. In 1852, two years after California went from being part of Mexico to part of the United States, Johnson cleared a rudimentary road between Placerville and Lake Tahoe, known as Johnson's Cut-Off. It followed the approximate route of today's U.S. Highway 50 until entering the Tahoe Basin. There it turned abruptly southeast through what is now called Christmas Valley and crossed Luther Pass, named for Ira Luther, who traveled by way of the pass in 1854 and painted his name on a rock, to meet the original emigrant trail at Hope Valley.

In the summer of 1853 Johnson and a correspondent for the *Placerville Herald* became the first white men of record to discover Meeks Bay. Washoes were living there, utilizing the lake, meadow, and stream that fed both. Nine miles directly across the lake they saw Cave Rock. Without explaining how they were able to understand the Washoe language, they reported that a centenarian patriarch told an ancient legend concerning the rock and a water prison of demons. The Americans claimed that the tale explained the wailings and pent-up moaning that could be heard increasing in terror and intensity when the waters of the lake rose. The incredibility of the entire episode is demonstrated by the description of the explorers' trip in hollowed-out logs across the lake to the granite massif. The cave, in the middle of the formation, is eighteen feet wide and ten feet high at its mouth and extends horizontally thirty feet to its eight-by-eight-foot back wall. In Johnson's tale it is described as a mysterious grotto two hundred feet high, full of icicles and stalactites.

More accurate descriptions of the area came from George H. Goddard, the surveyor for the California state boundary survey party, who in 1855 described Cave Rock simply as a "Legendary Cave." His comprehensive report on the lake's environs reads in part, "The surrounding mountains are three and perhaps four thousand feet above the lake, which is deep blue and perfectly fresh. The bases of the high mountain ranges are of white granite sand, forming beautiful beaches, and dense pine forests at other points run from the water's edge to the summit." He concluded his essay with an apologia: "My poor attempts with pencil can give but a faint idea of the beauty of this spot, and we can only hope to recall to those whose eyes have already beheld the scene what must ever be one of memory's most pleasant pictures."

Asa H. Hawley was one of the first Americans to settle at the south shore of the lake in the area pioneers called Lake Valley, later named

Meeks Bay, called Meigg's Bay when it was photographed in 1886. (Courtesy Special Collections, University of Nevada, Reno, Library)

Tahoe Valley. In 1854 he opened a trading post and public house along the Johnson route after he and two associates, the future railroad magnate Collis Huntington and James H. Nevett—later chairman of California's Wagon Road Directors—improved the Johnson roadway. Hawley's dealings with the Washoes at Tahoe were quite different from Johnson's. The Natives would not allow Hawley or other white men to fish in the lake. Hawley, who said he considered all Indians deceitful, said, "They tried to drive me off but I never was afraid of Indians except their treachery."

In either 1856 or 1857, Hawley, James Green, and John A. "Snowshoe" Thompson rowed a small boat that Hawley built around the lake, becoming the first Americans to navigate it. They were trying to discover if the lake had an outlet, an open question at that time. They discovered the Truckee, although they did not know its name. At one point, with Green rowing close to the shore, Hawley paced a half mile to see how fast they were traveling. They were trying to determine how long it would take them to circumvent the lake. Their primitive calculations lacked precision, and they concluded that Tahoe's circumference was 150 miles, more than twice its actual size.

In 1859 Capt. J. H. Simpson, of the U.S. Army Corps of Topographical Engineers, explored the Great Basin of the Utah Territory, much of which later became the state of Nevada. Coming upon Tahoe, then known as Lake Bigler, after John Bigler, California's twice-elected governor, Simpson described it as "a noble sheet of water . . . beautifully embosomed in the Sierra." On June 13 he wrote of a ride he had taken that morning: "Lake Valley is like a beautiful park, studded with large, stately pines. The glades between the trees are beautifully green, and the whole is enlivened by a pure, babbling mountain stream [the Upper Truckee River]. . . . The pines of various kinds are very large, and attain a height of probably from 100 to 150 feet. Their diameter is not infrequently as much as 8 feet, and they sometimes attain the dimension of 10 feet."

The Lake Tahoe described by the explorers, which generations of Washoes had known, soon changed; barbed wire, clear-cut forests, and tourist resorts became commonplace in the valley. The Americans denied the Indians access to the parts of the lake and its tributaries where fish were abundant. Tourists were catching hundreds of silver trout daily,

Datsolalee's masterful baskets were created after she saw them in dreams. (Courtesy Special Collections, University of Nevada, Reno, Library)

and commercial fishermen used half-mile-long seines to remove the fish by the ton, until eventually the lake's species was destroyed. As more and more Americans arrived, restrictions became more pronounced. In the last part of the twentieth century, elder Belma Jones commented on the privatization of the land: "We used to swim anywhere, and there weren't any houses, you know, on the beach like now. We used to go from the north shore clear over to what is now that estate there [Valhalla, on the south shore]. . . . Later people began to fence, so we couldn't go through there anymore."

Washoes managed to adapt, returning each summer to the lake, but now they worked as laborers, dairy hands, or domestics, setting up campsites in places no one else had claimed. Some men worked leading pack trips or as fishing and hunting guides; women turned from weaving utilitarian baskets to selling decorative baskets to tourists. The weavers, masters of perspective and symmetry, were among the best in the world. Gaining particular posthumous fame are Datsolalee, known not merely as an artist but as a genius, and her cousin Ceese; although not as prolific, she was thought by early-day collectors to be in every way equal to Datsolalee. The basket makers collected branches and roots from Tahoe's willow, cedar, fir, and pine and cured them for warping strands and dyes.

Datsolalee cured some materials for twelve years before using them. She saw baskets in her dreams and then produced them, using fine, even stitching and harmonious colors and designs. One of her most famous baskets, which took two years to make, contains 84,500 tightly woven stitches. Her baskets, as well as those of other Washoes, are now displayed in museums across the country, including the Steinbach Indian Basket Museum attached to the Gatekeeper's Museum at Tahoe City.

To this day the Washoe Indian legacy remains primarily historical at the lake, as the tribe owns no land. In 1998 the tribe won a competitive bid for a special-use permit to operate Meeks Bay Resort and Marina for up to thirty years. Another permit, for the same amount of time, was issued so they might manage a 350-acre meadow near the mouth of Meeks Creek for the care and harvesting of traditional plants. In August 2003 an act signed into law conveyed twenty-four acres on the east shore near Skunk Harbor to the secretary of the interior in trust for Washoe tribal uses. Although gaining access to these pieces of land, and having Washoe displays at D. L. Bliss State Park on the west shore and the Tallac Historic Site on the south, Washoes live primarily on reservations outside the Tahoe Basin. Since they had prospered in the lake's environs over a time span counted in thousands of years, it is apparent that their absence has been injurious to the welfare of both the tribe and the lake.

Chapter Two

Trails to Roads

*J*ames Sisson's lower legs were badly discolored: The gangrene had begun spreading upward from his feet. Unless his legs were amputated, he would die. Snow had trapped him in the Lake Valley cabin that served as a summer trading post between the two high passes on Johnson's Cut-Off. But on December 29, 1856, there were no other humans anywhere in the vicinity. He had baling rope and an ax, and he was contemplating forming tourniquets with the rope and attempting to cut off his legs. Caught by a blizzard, his boots had frozen to his frostbitten feet. He suffered through four days at the cabin without a fire. When he finally found matches under some scattered straw, he thawed the boots enough to remove them. Now, another eight days had passed, and Sisson dragged himself about, subsisting on raw flour left at the post.

Snowshoe Thompson, arguably the greatest mountaineer in Sierra history, had just begun a mail service that would last twenty years. He was crossing the mountains alone, carrying the mail on his back. Using oak slabs, he had fashioned ten-foot, twenty-five-pound skis after those he remembered from his early childhood in Norway. The trek from Placerville to Carson Valley and back consisted of 180 miles up and over the snow-filled mountains. On that December night he paused at the trading post and found Sisson. Thompson left the injured man, skiing through the night over Luther Pass to the nearest settlement, Genoa, Nevada. He recruited six men and guided the party back to the trading post.

They built a hand sled to carry the victim, but the travel was brutal. Snow had continued, adding two feet to the eight-foot snowpack, and only Thompson had much experience on skis. The sled, under Sisson's weight, sank, at times becoming buried almost out of sight. It took two days to get Sisson out of the mountains. In the valley they took him to the territory's only doctor, C. D. Daggett, who lived at the base of a mountain grade called Daggett Pass. The doctor knew he would have to amputate but needed chloroform. Thompson, without sleep, started out again, crossing the mountains to Sacramento and returning to Genoa some days later. Dr. Daggett performed the long-delayed operation, allowing Sisson to live many more years. Thompson carried the mail over the mountains every winter until 1876. For those twenty years, when the Sierra roads were buried in snow, he provided the only mail service between California and the East.

The harshness of the winters and the absence of developed roads caused other heartrending incidents. The most famous, the Donner Party episode, occurred in 1846. Stranded at the lake that now bears its

Above Donner Lake the daunting Sierra blocked emigrant wagon trains, leading to the Donner Party tragedy. (Courtesy Special Collections, University of Nevada, Reno, Library)

name, a number of the party cannibalized others who died from starvation and the elements. Although recently contested, distinguished Sierra historians George Hinkle and Bliss Hinkle wrote, "[Donner Party leader James F.] Reed himself, although he avoided mentioning names, left no doubt that there had been cannibalism."

Two years earlier, at the same spot, Moses Schallenberger, a twenty-year-old from the Elisha Stevens emigrant train, remained with two older men to guard wagons that had to be left behind. When storm followed violent storm and provisions dwindled, the men made makeshift snowshoes out of wagon bows and rawhide and started out. The older men fought their way over the pass and down into California; Schallenberger's strength gave out, and he was forced to return to the makeshift cabin they had built. He suffered through a miserable two months until help arrived, surviving by trapping a few foxes and almost inedible coyotes.

When a rescue averted a near tragedy at Tahoe, it led to a temporary name for the lake and a prolonged controversy. Explorer Frémont had wanted it called "Lake Bonpland," after an eminent French botanist, but his reports listed it as "Mountain Lake." In 1852 John Bigler led a party into Lake Valley to rescue snowbound emigrants. At the time, the man some referred to as "Honest John" was the governor of California, a position he held from 1852 to 1858, and it was suggested the lake be named Bigler.

Although loved by some, as his terms progressed, Bigler became hated by many. He commonly took action and, after the fact, challenged the legislature to pass measures to bring it into compliance with the state constitution. His popularity plummeted further as a habit of excessive use of intoxicants was attributed to him. Regarding naming the lake for him, historian H. H. Bancroft commented, "Nothing could have been in worse taste . . . than in applying to a liquid so beautifully clear and cool the name of one who so detested water." When Bigler's sympathy for the Southern cause and supposed support of the "Pacific Confederacy" became known, a serious movement demanded there be no "Copperhead" names on the state's landmarks.

Unionists William Van Wagener from New York, Judge Seneca Dean, and his nephew Robert Garwood Dean were partners in Lake House,

Tahoe's first shoreline hostelry on the south shore. Wanting the name of the lake changed, they obtained the Lake Valley Post Office under the name Tahoe, perhaps the Americanization of Daowaga—the Washoe Indian name. Later they convinced residents on the north shore, at the headwaters of the Truckee River, to call their settlement Tahoe City.

In 1862, with the Civil War raging, the U.S. General Land Office changed the lake's name to Tahoe. This did not stop California and Nevada legislators and newspaper editors, as well as various map-makers, from using their own judgment in references to the lake. In 1863 the *Washoe Times* insisted Bigler was appropriate for the body of water until "a lake of beer is discovered." Late that summer the eminent pastor Thomas Starr King visited the lake, gaining inspiration and using Tahoe in one of his most famous sermons, "Living Waters from Lake Tahoe." Early in the dispute, the pro-Union Republicans supported the change from Bigler, while pro-Southern Democrats argued against it. In 1870 the California legislature, controlled by Democrats, officially recognized the name Bigler. With the issue utterly confused, contentiousness between California and Nevada, racist attitudes toward Indians, misinformation, and sarcasm colored the ongoing argument. Public use of the name Tahoe eventually overcame all other factors. But it was not until 1945 that California's legislature rescinded the statute that had legalized Bigler, allowing the state to officially recognize the name Lake Tahoe.

Another tragic episode in the Sierra near Tahoe delayed the discovery of the Comstock Lode. In 1857 the Grosh brothers, the most scientific of all Nevada prospectors, discovered Sun Mountain's rich silver veins. They had been systematically surveying the area since 1852. In their cabin below the lode, they had a large technical library, a patent furnace, and an assaying laboratory. After they made their find, their luck ran out. Hosea Grosh struck his foot with a pick. The wound became infected, and he died shortly thereafter.

Six weeks later, on November 20, Ethan Allen Grosh and a friend, Richard Bucke, carrying ore samples, claims, charts, and assay reports, climbed into the Sierra, making their way toward California. They circled the north side of the lake, attempting to leave the basin through Squaw Valley. Sheets of rain and snowy blizzards stopped them. Lost and suffering, they shot their mule for food and tossed away their soaked heavy coats and ore samples, hiding the secret claims and assays in a fallen tree. Pressing on, at one point they found human tracks, only to realize they were their own; they had been walking in a circle.

After Grosh and Bucke wandered about for two weeks, close to death from hunger and exposure, Mexican miners found them. The miners saved Bucke's life by amputating his leg and other foot using a hunting knife and saw. Grosh died delirious, talking of the silver veins. After recuperating, Bucke turned his back on the Comstock, returning to his home in Canada and becoming one of that country's leading medical men.

In June 1859 others stumbled upon the Grosh brothers' discovery. That winter news spread throughout California, and as soon as melting snows allowed, the rush began. The strike, called the Comstock Lode, turned out to be the richest in the world. Getting at the Comstock ore, as in some developing California mines, required a completely different system than the placer mining done by the forty-niners. The veins went down many hundreds of feet. Whereas the early-day miners had panned for "color" in streams or dug for it with shovels on hillsides, mines on the Comstock needed large numbers of day-wage laborers who worked deep underground. The hard-rock mining required great amounts of capital for wages and building infrastructure, regardless of whether a mine worked in pay ore. The new mining mirrored the era's Gilded Age phenomenon of corporations replacing family farms and local businesses. Syndicates were needed to raise money, and investors created a stock market in San Francisco where speculators could gamble on investments in the mines. The new industry led to the hurried development of Lake Tahoe and the destruction of its forests.

Previously, the roadway from Placerville was little more than a beaten path through old-growth forest inhabited by wolves and bears. Accounts of hazards and accidents were commonplace, including the sudden appearance of a grizzly that caused horses pulling a stage to bolt, snapping their traces and toppling the coach.

With the discovery of the Comstock Lode, transportation to Virginia City became of critical importance. Packing services and stage lines vied with one another to provide the fastest service. The counties of Sacramento and El Dorado, through which the road east ran, had begun improving the road in the late 1850s, each using assessments of $25,000 for road construction. When the California government advanced a policy that allowed toll roads to be built over particularly difficult or hazardous portions of the line, or where bridges or shortcuts would be advantageous, access quickly improved.

People scrambled to secure way stations and toll-road rights. Mere weeks after the lode's discovery, turnouts on the road were filled with merchants providing food and liquor to the steady stream of people making their way to the Comstock. Before the end of the season, makeshift shelters were added so travelers could spend the night. There were three toll roads between Placerville and Lake Tahoe and at least two between the lake and Carson Valley at the base of the Sierra's eastern crest. Beginning in the summer of 1859, all manner of supplies and goods were carried ashore from the river at Sacramento and hauled over the turnpike to Virginia City. An endless array of goods, everything from grain and canned goods to bricks, finished lumber, and mining machinery, was carted, drawn, or dragged to Nevada.

Wagons crossing the Sierra in early spring. (Courtesy Special Collections, University of Nevada, Reno, Library)

Inez Veerkamp, a descendant of pioneer farmers, reported, "I remember Father talking about the difficult times they had getting over [Johnson Pass]. Grandfather hauled by horses, mules, and wagons then. That would have been in 1860. The road was nothing but a dirt trail over the summit. They made overnight stops at Kyburz, Pacific House, and Strawberry. The stopping places would be crowded with animals, wagons, and people." By August 1860, on one peak day, 353 wagons made their way along the trail. Teamsters reported that in traversing the road, "a bottle always helped."

Road builders developed the Lake Tahoe Wagon Road in 1860, and it became one of the busiest thoroughfares in the West. The new route came down Johnson Grade into Lake Valley and followed a trail along the lake's south shore, leaving the valley by way of a section of toll road over Kingsbury Grade. Named for one of the road's builders, who claimed to have spent $15,000 on its construction, Kingsbury followed the route over what had been known as Daggett Pass. Charges to use the new pass were the most expensive on the entire road, $2.50 and $0.25 for each extra animal. The new route became the preferred roadway, cutting

Halting for the night on the Lake Tahoe Wagon Road, one of the busiest thoroughfares in the West. (Courtesy Special Collections, University of Nevada, Reno, Library)

seventeen miles from the old route over Luther Pass. Lake Valley way stations, hostelries, barns, and stables mushroomed, becoming a prominent part of the road in the valley.

In 1851 Martin Smith had established a backcountry wilderness post at the base of Johnson Grade, making him the first white settler at Tahoe. He was a trapper and a trader who stayed at the lake throughout the summer, advertising with a crude handmade sign: "Groceries—Meals at All Hours—and Lodging If Required." In 1853 Smith attempted to stimulate interest in the lake valley by reporting a gold strike in an article in the *Placerville Herald.* After the opening sentence the article said nothing further of the strike but instead touted the wonders of the lake's "amazing grottos" and the valley's "strawberries in August." The article served its purpose, attracting adventurers, not all of them welcome. In 1855 two notorious California murderers, Mickey Free and George Wilson, killed two trading-post owners and set fire to the handful of way stations in the basin. Smith survived, but his post was burned to the ground. He rebuilt the following year, and in 1857 his new hostelry served as a horse-change station for the first stagecoach line over the summits between Placerville and Genoa. In the summer of 1859 Smith sold out to Ephraim "Yank" Clement and his wife, Lydia, known to all as "Aunt Liddy."

The Clements expanded the way station, and it quickly became the most successful of the early hostelries in the basin. Yank, a portly, gregarious teller of tall tales, promoted a mountain-man image by keeping his curly hair long and wearing buckskins and moccasins. He also provided a meal and a place to sleep to travelers, whether they could pay or not. Aunt Liddy, as reserved as Yank was sociable, ministered to the sick, practiced midwifery, and tended to those in need of domestic counseling.

Yank's Station, later known as Meyers, featured corrals for two hundred animals, two saloons, a general store, a blacksmith shop, a cooperage, and what Yank built into a three-story, fourteen-room inn. When fortune seekers suggested Yank join them in procuring some of the plentiful silver in Virginia City, he replied, "My silver's here, right under my feet, on the Great Bonanza Road." Years later the Clements changed locations, moving to the lakefront, continuing to run hostelries at Tahoe until Yank's death in the mid-1890s. For more than thirty years he maintained his reputation as "the best-liked host in the Sierra."

Another of the first hostelries built along the Tahoe Wagon Road was called Sierra House. Robert Dean built it on the edge of an extensive meadow overlooking Cold Creek in 1858. When the Comstock rush began in earnest, Dean sold the site to join his uncle in ownership of the imposing Lake House on Tahoe's shore. Sierra House sold again in 1867 and again in 1871. The halfway station rounding the lake, Sierra House featured five rooms downstairs, other accommodations upstairs, a saloon, and a covered porch fronting the road and running the length of the building. It had four large barns, stables, and a stock corral. Its owners grew hay in the surrounding acreage and ran cattle in High Meadows, uphill to the east.

"Long-Haired Sam" Brown, a notorious killer, frequented the Sierra House saloon, intimidating defenseless customers. Also known on the Comstock and in Carson Valley, Brown was said to have used both gun and knife to kill any number of men. Although called "Fighting" Brown, he generally killed in cowardly fashion when the victim's back was turned. He bragged about keeping his own private cemetery. Brown became the victim himself when his attempt to assassinate unarmed Carson Valley rancher Henry Van Sickle failed in July 1861. Van Sickle secured a shotgun, chased the outlaw down, and killed him. The coroner's finding concluded, "Samuel Brown has come to his death from a just dispensation of an all wise providence."

The acknowledged heroes of the era were the teamsters. Those who knew cited "Curly Bill" Gerhart as the best, but "Big John" Littlefield, Ned Blair, Charlie Watson, and "Baldy" Green—who held the record for being stopped by the most road agents—were not far behind. The most famous driver was Hank Monk, who became a legend because his stories equaled his driving prowess, and his drinking surpassed both. One report from Glenbrook, on Tahoe's east shore, said Monk was "so full of liquor that he couldn't stand, but he could drive all right." One of his tall tales told of Monk having invested in the winter mining of trout at Emerald Bay. He told the *Carson Appeal* he expected lucrative dividends as long as the cold weather held. Miners, he said, were busy driving shafts and winzes through the ice at the lake to capture the fish that were "fixed like bees in drops of amber."

Monk became a national folk hero by driving Horace "Go West

Young Man" Greeley from Genoa through Lake Valley to Placerville. Greeley, getting a late start, needed to arrive by five o'clock for a speaking engagement. Assuring his passenger he would get him there on time, Monk urged his horses forward at a breakneck pace, pausing only to change teams. The vehicle flew up and down the Carson Spur and over the Sierra crest. At one juncture Monk described looking back at the candidate, "his bare head bobbing, sometimes on the back and then on the front of the seat, sometimes in the coach and then out, and then on the top and then on the bottom, holding on to whatever he could grab." With the coach taking corners on two wheels high above the American River, Greeley called out that an hour or two probably would not make that much of a difference. Monk replied, "Horace, keep your seat! I told you I would get you there by five o'clock, and by God I'll do it . . . if the axles hold." Greeley arrived on time, and the story gained a life of its own. By the time humorist Artemus Ward and his associate Mark Twain finished dressing it up, everyone in the country had heard the tale, and most had repeated it, including New York congressman Calvin Hulburd, one of Greeley's political opponents, who read humorist Ward's account into the *Congressional Record.*

Unlike the thoroughfare in and out of the valley, the east and west shore roads around the lake remained undeveloped. The area produced resources, in particular fish and hay, which when baled as feed sold for $250 a ton. The necessity of getting goods to market required that lake craft change dramatically from the Washoe Indians' dugouts and the backcountry woodsmen's homemade skiffs. In the spring of 1860, Al L. Fish and William S. Ferguson built the schooner *Iron Duke* and launched it at the outlet to the Truckee on the northwest shore, near what is now the Gatekeeper's Museum and Fanny Bridge in Tahoe City. The *Iron Duke* transported the hay to the south shore for sale to those on the Lake Tahoe Wagon Road or to Glenbrook, on the east shore, for shipment to Virginia City.

Three years later William Pomin surveyed the land on the shore above the *Iron Duke* launch site, established Tahoe City, and built the Tahoe House Inn. At that time Pomin's wife gave birth to a daughter, named Tahoe: the first American girl born at the lake. A month or two after her birth her mother, demonstrating pioneer hardiness, took Tahoe on mule back to their former home, Forest Hills, returning the same day—a sixty-mile trek.

The *Iron Duke* was an impressive sixty-foot schooner that had an eighteen-foot beam and two masts that were forty-two and forty-eight feet high. The sturdy double-ender could tote 125 tons of hay, and although carrying passengers when room allowed, it made hay-loading stops as it sailed along the east or west shore.

The *Edith Batty* also sailed Tahoe in the early 1860s. Described as a "slow-moving sloop," it served as the first mail and supply carrier, stopping at settlements around the lake. It took a full week for the *Edith Batty* to make the seventy-two-mile trip, and it followed an irregular schedule. A gregarious San Franciscan named Ramsdale Buoy, who visited the lake in 1866, described the windjammer's long sweep oars for use when becalmed, which, he noted, "appeared to be a majority of the time."

George "Little Dock" Gordinier hauled two twenty-eight-foot whaleboats in the procession over Johnson Pass during the rush of 1860. One of the massive and unwieldy loads was delivered to William W. "Billy" Lapham, a New England seafarer, who used it beginning in August 1860 for commercial fishing. He netted thousands of native silver and

cutthroat trout for sale at Lapham's Fish Market and Landing, through which the south shore state-line boundary ran.

The other whaler had been ordered by Rufus Walton, who with Capt. Augustus W. Pray and two others established Glenbrook, first known as Walton's Landing, for enterprises originating at the site. After selling his interest in the landing in 1863, Walton developed a toll road over what became Spooner Summit. He sold the road's rights within a year and disappeared from Tahoe history, leaving only the soon-to-be-eclipsed place-names Walton Landing and Walton Road.

After buying out Walton and several less-remembered partners, former sea captain Pray built a home and ranch, thirty cottages, a horse livery, a butcher shop, and—on pilings over the water—a general store with a dance hall in its second story. Pray's enterprises included planting potatoes and barley, which reports said "cannot be excelled by the lowlands of the far distant Sacramento." But Pray's activity that had the greatest ramifications was his establishment of a shoreline lumber mill, housing a steam-powered set of double circular saws. Tahoe's first timber barons would begin their operations by buying and expanding the mill. While gaining wealth that eventually equaled that of the Comstock silver kings, the timber men's enterprises were ruinous to the environment, denuding Tahoe's mountains and spoiling the clarity of the lake.

Chapter Three

Timber

*D*uring the last quarter of the nineteenth century, the driving force of forest management was the production of commercial timber. The doctrine of multiple use was one hundred years away. No consideration was given the role of undisturbed woodlands in erosion control or providing plant biodiversity or wildlife habitat. Human recreation in the form of sports hunting was pursued in certain areas by wealthy Comstockers, but the removal of the basin's trees for use in the mines ensured the activity had no long-term future.

Before the forests' demise, the *Ursus arctos horribilis,* or grizzly, was the king of beasts in America. Like the extermination of wolves, that of the grizzly in California was only a matter of time; the last died in 1922. Both wolf and grizzly were seen as vermin, useless and a threat to humans as well as livestock. A federal eradication policy that included trapping and poisoning eliminated the wolves in almost all of the lower forty-eight states. Grizzly bears fell mainly to sport hunting, the nineteenth century's quintessential sport. From the time of Lewis and Clark's expedition, it became almost a rite of passage for explorers and frontiersmen to kill and be attacked by bears. Davy Crockett became the "Coonskin Congressman" in large part because of his reputation as an indefatigable bear hunter. Among those mauled by grizzlies were Daniel Boone, Jedediah Smith, and several fur traders, including Hugh Glass, and one of the Sublette brothers, Andrew, who died of his wounds. Hunter-heroes were popular in literature as well, beginning with James Feni-more Cooper's Leatherstocking in 1823.

Several grizzly-bear traits ensured their overkilling. They stood from six to twelve feet tall, and many were well over five hundred pounds. They exhibited terrible rage when roused, and, adding to the thrill, if wounded, they moved toward the place from which the shot came. Hunting them became one of the ultimate sport challenges.

In the mid-1860s, with an absence of government regulation, Lake Tahoe's meadows began hosting sheep and dairy cattle. The sedentary prey attracted grizzlies, which in turn brought additional pressure for their extermination.

At the lake the killing of a grizzly made the hunter a cause célèbre. "Big Jim" Small claimed to have killed a grizzly near Kingsbury Grade that ran fourteen hundred pounds with a paw print that "exceeded the size of a Westphalia ham," and George "Grizzly" Davis had eleven griz-zly skulls on his fence railing. But the most famous of the grizzly hunt-ers was six-foot-six John Washington McKinney, a mountain man with no formal education for whom McKinney Creek and Bay are named. The area had been valuable to the Washoes for fishing and collecting medicinal plants, as well as *mugaulu,* a plant whose root had magical efficacy in deer hunting. Whether McKinney used the root or not, begin-ning in 1862 he made his reputation leading Comstock mine owners and other huntsmen into the tall timber from his resort, "Hunter's Retreat." Dressed in moccasins and fringed buckskin, he used his Sharps buffalo rifle when tracking grizzly.

One bear McKinney did not kill was the lake's legendary giant, "Old Brin," named for his brindled color. Reports had him attacking livestock and threatening humans beginning with the white man's arrival at Lake Tahoe. Old Brin was described by one mountain man as "nearly one ton of bear." It lost two toes on its right foot escaping the trap of Grizzly Davis, who gave the bear its name. Settlers saw Old Brin in many Tahoe locales throughout the years and, befitting its legendary status, some-times in several places at the same time.

In 1881, twenty-some years after first being identified, Old Brin mauled and devoured a sheepherder above Sugar Pine Point on the west shore. The tree in which the man sought refuge had been stripped of its bark to a height of nearly nine feet. Mountain men who first discovered the gruesome scene identified the bear by its track: eleven inches across and fourteen in length, with two toes on its right foot missing. The group tracked the bear, believing "we're next if we don't get him." In heavy manzanita above Rubicon Point, they got a shot, but missed—and Old Brin disappeared into history.

The grizzly-bear species would have had at least a chance of surviving the sportsmen if Americans had not destroyed its habitat as well. Unfortunately for all animals at Lake Tahoe, young German immigrant Phillipp Deidesheimer invented square-sets as a means of securing the mines of Virginia City. The sets, built inside the ever-deepening tunnels, were quadrangles of twelve-inch-square posts, six feet high and five feet long. Notches cut in the upper end of each post allowed four additional posts to rest upon it or connect alongside it. In this fashion an interlocking system of sets could be expanded in any direction. Because it secured each foot of the ever-deepening tunnels and caverns of ore, the system required unimaginable quantities of lumber.

In much the same way it had done for settlers with the Homestead Act and miners with the Mineral Resources Act and General Mining Law, Congress in effect subsidized the timber industry by allowing it unlimited access to the resource. Originally under the Pacific Railway Act of 1862 and later the Timber and Stone Act of 1878, public domain forests were sold for nominal fees.

In 1872 three men from the Comstock's infamous Bank Ring monopoly—D. L. Bliss, a Virginia City banker; Henry M. Yerington, director of the Virginia and Truckee Railroad; and D. O. Mills, who was one of three original Bank Ring members and later erected the largest office building in New York City—joined to form the Carson and Tahoe Lumber and Fluming Company. After acquiring seven thousand acres of timber along the lake's south shore for next to nothing, they bought up much of Pray's settlement and expanded the milling operation.

Like other fledgling Tahoe logging operations, the Carson and Tahoe Lumber and Fluming Company brought in lumberjacks, a good many from Canada. In most operations the men worked in units: two sawyers, a swamper, a chainer, and a teamster in charge of an oxen team. The sawyers used two-man crosscut saws to fell trees and buck them up, cutting them into ten- to sixteen-foot lengths. The swamper cut the limbs from the tree and cleared the brush from the path of the teamster and his animals. The chainer connected the heavy link chain from the lengths of timber to the yoke of the oxen, and the team pulled the logs to the head of log chutes or flumes, inclined channels of water, where horses would drag or gravity would propel the logs out of the stand of timber.

Sawyers had to be imported because their work required not only strength and stamina but also great skill. They had to drop each tree in a specific direction between others in the stand. One of the sawyers would notch the log in the direction of the fall, and they would saw from the opposite side above the level of the notch. When the tree was cut nearly through, the weakened core could not hold it, and the tree would fall over the notch.

If felled incorrectly, the tree would hang up on the branches of nearby trees or end up propped against another. To drop such a tree necessitated cutting the one blocking its fall. A tree cut through but still standing or leaning was called a "widow maker," because of the tendency for it to crash down at any time while the sawyers were working to free it. Lumberjacks, circa 1880, were generally paid $20 to $50 a month, with swampers getting the least and sawyers the most. But a newsman in the town of Truckee, twelve miles north of the lake on the river of the same name, reported that in the Tahoe area's multimillion-dollar industry, woodsmen were getting $70 or even as much as $150 a month.

The Carson and Tahoe Company soon included short-line railroads on the south shore, carrying timber down the mountainsides to the lake. Steamer ships met the cars at the end of long piers at Camp Richardson or Bijou. Using one-hundred-foot barges, the company towed its cargo across the water to Glenbrook, where the shoreline sawmills drew the timber directly from the water onto saw carriages. The most prominent of the hauling craft was the iron-hulled *Meteor,* which towed thousands of logs between 1876 and 1896. It was so powerful that under a tow of three hundred thousand feet of saw logs, it could still cruise with most of the steamers on Tahoe. When no longer needed to lug timber, the *Meteor* remained a familiar sight on the lake, serving until 1928 as a passenger liner in summer and a mail carrier in winter.

Once the logs were cut into the desired lengths at Glenbrook, another

A Carson and Tahoe Company train hauling timber up logged mountainsides to the summit to be carried by flume out of the mountains. (Courtesy Special Collections, University of Nevada, Reno, Library)

short line transported them to the summit. The trains wound their way nine miles up Spooner Grade, crossing ten trestles and passing through a 487-foot tunnel. At Spooner Summit, as atop other accessible points, flumes, formed of two-inch planks shaped like the letter V sitting atop trestle works, carried the logs and lumber out of the mountains. The flumes were up to twelve miles long and cost as much as $500,000 to construct.

The flumes above Glenbrook were largely tended by Chinese workers who had formerly worked building the Central Pacific Railroad. Working for the railroad, they proved to be industrious and daring, in some instances dangling in baskets two thousand feet above the American River gorge to chisel the roadway through granite. Tending the flumes and cutting cord wood, they lived in some fifty isolated enclaves, preserving as much of their culture, especially in food and medicine, as possible. Prevented from bringing their families to America, and with interracial marriage forbidden, the bachelors lived in small groups. The largest group lived in Glenbrook, where their fresh vegetable gardens were renowned, and some worked at the hotel.

Because Chinese customs and language were alien to whites and because white jobs were lost to Chinese laborers, who were paid about half the wages of whites, antagonistic relations between the groups prevailed. In 1882 anti-Chinese agitation in the West instigated the passage of the Chinese Exclusion Act, and as the logging business declined, there were few jobs to keep them at the lake. Some probably moved to cities: San Francisco, Sacramento, Reno, and Placerville, all of which had substantial Chinese populations. Others may have moved to boomtowns that needed labor. Across the lake in Truckee, a town of railroaders and lumberjacks, a Chinese community of some one thousand was forced from the area in the mid-1880s when the Caucasian League burned down their cabins, shot to death one man as he ran, and wounded another.

At the same time the Carson and Tahoe Lumber and Fluming Company was prospering at Glenbrook, Walter Scott Hobart and his general manager, Capt. John Bear Overton, established the Sierra Nevada Wood and Lumber Company on the north shore. Hobart had served in various public offices in Nevada, including that of state controller. An associate of the mining magnate John Mackay, he served as president of the water company that built a pipeline from Marlette Lake in the Sierra to bring fresh water to Virginia City. Overton worked for Hobart as the superintendent of the water company. He later created the first electrically powered process mill on the Comstock to work its low-grade ore.

Hobart acquired ten thousand acres of forestland. In an area heavily used by the Washoe Indians because of its abundance of all types of berries, Overton engineered a nearly vertical four-thousand-foot double-track, narrow-gauge tramline. It was called the Great Incline of the Sierra Nevada, its base located at what is now Incline Village. Lengths of timber, rafted by steamer from the southeast shore, were hauled by yoked oxen from the lake at Sand Harbor and carried by locomotives to a little mill town and the Great Incline sawmill. The timber was milled and then run on a short-spur track to join the tramline at its base. The tram could carry three hundred cords of wood or its equivalent in lumber to the summit to be fed into a V flume and carried down the other side of the mountain on its way to the Comstock.

Flumes could be as high as seventy feet above the ground. A steady

stream of water carried the lengths of timber thousands of feet, while the steep grades prevented logjams. Daredevils sometimes rode down flumes for excitement. On one occasion a reporter rode with two of the Comstock's richest bonanza kings, James Flood, builder of San Francisco's Flood Building and Flood Mansion, and "Slippery" Jim Fair, for whom San Francisco's Fairmont Hotel is named.

The two "boats" were sixteen feet long and V-shaped to match the flume. Each had an end board at the rear of the craft so the current would propel it along. As the boats touched the water, the men awkwardly boarded and were hurled forward. They could not stop; they could not lessen the speed. The ride lasted some thirty minutes. At the steepest grades water cascaded upon them so furiously it became impossible to see ahead. At lesser grades the view, twenty, thirty, forty feet or more above the earth, terrified the reporter. The steepest declination, estimated to be forty-five degrees, made the boat seem merely to fall, and the reporter, unable to take a breath, thought he would suffocate. At the terminus the soaked riders disembarked "more dead than alive." The reporter said that the next day neither Flood nor Fair left his bed.

With the wood companies' development, heavy old-growth stands—containing massive cedar; "mammoth six and seven-foot-through sugar pine," called the pride of the California forests; and junipers, some as large as four feet through—were stripped from the land. In July 1873 the *Truckee Republican* reported that forty-man logging camps of French Canadian lumberjacks were averaging one tree dropped every three minutes, saying, "The great forest kings are crashing in every direction."

D. L. Bliss thought one tree his company cut was one thousand years old; it was eleven feet in diameter. By the end of the decade he noted, "Nearly everything around the lake is bought up or taken up. Until recently on the other side of the lake we have only taken such timbers as would make logs, but lately we have cleaned off not only what was fit for logs but what would make wood."

The destruction included more than stripping the hillsides. Log drives in the Truckee River, as well as the eastern slope's Carson River, caused riverbed diversions and pollution. As the towering growth that kept the forest floor cool and moist disappeared, so too did the varied species of animals dependent on it.

Tree roots had held stream banks and hillsides in place; any precipitation now carried the topsoil into the water. Stream temperatures rose, killing off fish. Logging debris, sawdust, and siltation filled in gravel beds that they depended on for spawning—including those in the Truckee River that had hosted the four-foot cutthroat trout. The bare hillsides meant early snowmelt so that streams flooded in spring and became trickles in late summer.

The ultimate result of the hurried clear-cutting was to reduce the timber industry's ability to conduct operations. As far back as 1876 the president of the American Geographical Society had announced that the "magnificent forests of Lake Tahoe . . . are being felled so rapidly to supply timber for the miners that in twelve years there will be no timber left for many miles." In 1881 a *Reno Evening Gazette*'s account noted the result of nearly twenty years of activity on that year's harvest: "Trees are scattered, and the work is expensive."

California state assemblyman James V. Coleman lamented the destruction of the forests and pushed through a resolution in 1883 that declared the state must protect what remained of Tahoe's natural scenery

for health, pleasure, and recreation. He headed a committee that proposed the state buy lands that were not owned by private entities and create a forestry commission. Officials agreed to create the new agency but rejected buying lands. The forestry commission issued reports on the damage of wasteful logging practices and unchecked fires and then dissolved in 1892. Cutting continued until the resource was depleted.

Over twenty-eight years, the most productive of the companies, the Carson and Tahoe Lumber and Fluming Company, took an estimated 750 million board feet of lumber and 500,000 cords of firewood from the Tahoe Basin. At the Incline, the Sierra Nevada Wood and Lumber Company's Hobart mills shut down in 1897, moving its hundreds of tons of machinery out of the basin to a new operation northwest of Truckee. The company left behind enormous piles of bark and sawdust and the deep scars of the logging roads. Its total production was estimated at 200 million board feet of lumber and more than 1 million cords.

On the south shore stumps of cutover land, discarded equipment, and logging waste were all that remained. Land sold for $1.50 an acre or less. Nearly 50,000 acres had been stripped, leaving barely 950 acres of pine stands. Old growth remained only in areas of extreme terrain or around scattered homes and resorts. Comstock historian Grant Smith commented, "No later visitor could conceive of the majesty and beauty fed into the maws of those voracious sawmills." Today the nineteenth century's massive undertaking is marked by the uniformity in size of the second-growth forests that surround the lake.

Chapter Four

Schemes and Schemers

$\mathcal{S}$imultaneous with the loggers' operations, other fortune seekers and entrepreneurs were scrambling to use the lake for their purposes. In 1862 the completion of the Walton Toll Road up Spooner Summit north of Cave Rock connected the Comstock and Carson City to Lake Tahoe. The following year the well-financed Lake Bigler Toll Road Company bought out Walton. The company proposed to join the Spooner Summit road with the Lake Tahoe Wagon Road south of the rock to better accommodate the wagons utilizing the thoroughfare. Spooner Summit was 150 feet lower than the previously preferred Carson link, Kingsbury Grade. The only impediment to what would become known as the "Bonanza Road" was the Washoe Indian sacred place, Cave Rock.

Builders widened the deer trail behind the massive feature, but heavier freighters had difficulty pulling the grade. Engineers then constructed a trestle to support a one-way wooden bridge on the lake side. Rough, quarried granite blocks were stacked and bolted to the rock face to sustain the structure. The construction of the approaches to it and the bridge cost the incredible sum of ten thousand dollars. The bridge's narrow, torturous planking stood seventy-five feet above the lake, a thin rail said to be the only thing between teamsters and eternity.

On the other side of the lake, the same summer, two prospectors, Shannon Knox and John Keiser, were meandering toward the Comstock when they found an outcropping of red ore across the Truckee

The Cave Rock trestle and wooden bridge seventy-five feet above the lake. (Courtesy Special Collections, University of Nevada, Reno, Library)

River from Squaw Valley. Times being what they were, within a month there were a thousand men, no women or children yet, living in tent, log, and brush structures around the idyllic tree-lined meadow near the outcropping or in other nearby camps. Known as Knoxville, the main "city" featured two hotels, a butcher shop, a shanty under a tree with a sign reading "Union Clothing Store," faro houses, and saloons. William Brewer, the first chair of agricultural studies at Yale University's Sheffield Scientific School, who wrote the classic *Up and Down California* and for whom a mountain in the southern Sierra is named, passed through Knoxville and noted the inhabitants' excitement but concluded, "I surely would not invest in any mine I have seen today, and I have visited eight or nine of the best."

Brewer's judgment proved correct, and the fortune seekers abandoned the site within a year. The camp is a significant footnote in Lake Tahoe history, though, as its phantom strike attracted a number of prominent settlers. They included John W. McKinney, William A. Barker, John Ward, H. C. Blackwood, and Dick Madden, each of whom homesteaded land in, near, or within eyesight of some west-shore valley, creek, bay, or peak to which his name became attached. William Pomin, who had also joined the rush, moved to the lakeshore and founded Tahoe City.

One might think William Ralston had been an early settler on the south shore, since a mountain peak, a lake, and a road atop Echo Summit, the old Johnson Grade, are named for him. But Ralston rarely left the San Francisco area except to check on investments. He wielded unlimited power on the West Coast in the 1860s and early '70s, founding the greatest financial institution in the West, the Bank of California. Ralston took risks lending bank money as well as his own and became known as "the man who built California."

It was Ralston who enlisted D. O. Mills and a failed real estate investor, William Sharon, to create the all-powerful Bank Ring on the Comstock. He was one of the founders of the Pacific Coast Stock Exchange and seemed involved in every other major early-day business on the coast. He listened to anyone with plans for advancing an enterprise. He bought hundreds of patents and provided money for everything from planting the first northern California vineyards to creating a California wool industry and building San Francisco's California Theater and the Palace Hotel. He invested heavily in the mines and mills of the Comstock, and in 1870 he and two partners acquired Tahoe's Glenbrook Hotel. When Ralston refused to allow a new city in central California to be named for him, the founders named it for his attribute: Modesto, Spanish for "modest."

Ralston's largesse finally broke him. When the mining stock market crashed in 1875, directors found that almost all of the Bank of California's reserves had been secretly used for investments in the mines or California businesses. As the bank verged on collapse, Ralston swam out into San Francisco Bay and drowned. Even knowledge of his illegal use of bank funds and apparent suicide did not dash his popularity. At his funeral San Franciscans filled the street for a mile, following behind his hearse.

In the fall of 1864 workers completed a wagon road north of Lake Tahoe. It followed the abandoned Truckee River route over Donner Pass, running between Sacramento and Virginia City. It was constructed to haul equipment and supplies to build the Central Pacific Railroad, which would follow the same line. The route had fallen into disuse in the 1850s because pioneer wagons had such difficulty crossing the pass from the steep east side to the west. Theodore Judah, the man who designed the trans-Sierra railroad route, chose the Truckee roadway because it would be the easiest for trains to cross using the long, gradual climb up from the west. Improved road construction and a large labor force of hard-working Chinese emigrants would overcome the east side's topography. The Truckee route also required crossing only one pass rather than the multiple passes, canyons, and severe undulations of other roads across the Sierra.

The new wagon road cost two hundred thousand dollars and took 350 men working ten months to complete. Its width, twenty feet, allowed travel in both directions at once, a great improvement over the Lake Tahoe Wagon Road and the Bonanza Road. It siphoned so much traffic from the south-shore route that opponents charged that the corporation's railroad proposal had been a subterfuge simply to gain government money for the profitable wagon thoroughfare. Of course, although making as much money as possible off the road, the Central Pacific magnates intended to carry their project to completion, knowing the railway would be many times more profitable.

It was in 1864 as well that A. W. Von Schmidt, the Prussian immigrant engineer who built San Francisco's first water supply system, quit his position at the city's monopolistic Spring Valley Water Company. He gave up his job, intending to build an aqueduct to utilize water from Lake Tahoe for California's burgeoning development. He formed a company called the Lake Tahoe and San Francisco Water Works, backed by several wealthy San Francisco entrepreneurs. Their proposal included draining up to five hundred million gallons from the lake per day during eight months of the year when Sierra creeks and streams that would feed his line did not produce that amount.

The water would be used by California cities and towns from Auburn to Benicia as well as to run the hydraulic mines in the California foothills, irrigate the Central Valley, and finally provide drinking water for San Francisco. The *San Francisco Morning Call* declared the plan "the most stupendous water works enterprise ever undertaken on the American continent." Virginia City's *Territorial Enterprise* immediately warned those entertaining such thoughts that they would need "twenty regiments of militia" to steal the pure waters of the bistate lake.

Von Schmidt wanted San Francisco to issue ten million dollars in bonds and petitioned the U.S. Congress to grant him rights-of-way for 163 miles of flumes, canals, tunnels, and pipes. In February 1870 he got a

Senate bill introduced to aid the project's construction. The plan was vigorously opposed by Nevada's legislature and California capitalists with Nevada interests, as well as local residents and groups of taxpayers who believed it reeked of corruption. A year later a bill in the House of Representatives opposed the proposed diversion.

Von Schmidt never acquired the necessary financial backing or the rights-of-way. When it appeared he would, in 1870, he constructed a timber crib dam, some three miles below the lake, to regulate the Truckee River. Guards were posted to protect it against "hot headed residents," by which was meant downstream farmers and mill owners. Nevada residents cried that Von Schmidt should "be the one damned."

Although Von Schmidt built the dam, the Donner Lumber and Boom Company, a subsidiary of the Central Pacific Railroad that had been awarded a twenty-year franchise for use of the Truckee River by the California legislature, also claimed ownership. The railroad company won, using the dam for many years to control the water flow and charging lumbermen to carry logs to mills in the town of Truckee.

While Von Schmidt's scheme was faltering, in 1873 the Lake Tahoe drainage began providing water to Virginia City and the Comstock

A. W. Von Schmidt's original timber crib dam on the Truckee River. (Courtesy Special Collections, University of Nevada, Reno, Library)

mines. Bonanza king John Mackay, Walter Hobart, and their associates funded the project of transporting mountain water twenty-five miles across the deep depression of Washoe Valley, an engineering feat never before attempted anywhere in the world. Previously, the greatest pressure under which water had been carried was 910 feet; the new pipe required withstanding 1,720 feet of pressure. Hermann Schussler, the young engineer who succeeded Von Schmidt at Spring Valley Water, superintended the construction.

In contrast to Von Schmidt's venture, this plan had little opposition, because instead of using Lake Tahoe's bistate water, it used Marlette Lake, above Tahoe at 8,000 feet and wholly in Nevada. (The man-made lake, as well as the creek that feeds it, is named for Seneca Hunt Marlette, California's surveyor general, who first mapped the area.) The head of Marlette Basin had already been dammed to a height of 26 feet. Its collected water was then conveyed six miles south by V flume to Spooner Summit, where it was stored to feed a twelve-mile V flume that carried timber down to Carson City.

The new project raised the dam at Marlette to stand 37 feet high. Auxiliary flumes collected water from numerous creeks on the side of the mountains and carried water east from Marlette to another storage reservoir leading to the seven-mile pipeline. It took almost a year to build the pipe that would carry the water down into and across Washoe Valley. Differing thicknesses of the rolled metal were needed depending on the perpendicular pressure and lateral curves designed to circumvent hills or rock outcroppings. Hydraulic engineers thought it impossible to move water so far under so much pressure. But the bold scheme set off cannons and rockets all over the high desert town when completed in August 1873, and the system continues to supply water to Virginia City in the twenty-first century.

A similar, though less venturesome, project took water from Echo Lake, above Tahoe's south shore, to supplement the waters of the South Fork of the American River for use in California. The river filled reservoirs for mining and drinking water. As with Marlette Lake, because this enterprise involved the watershed entirely in one state, it proceeded unchallenged. Over two summers a 1,056-foot tunnel was drilled through the granite below Echo Summit, and the lake was tapped in 1876. In the spring of 1911 the dam broke, causing a flood that swept down the summit, washing the Osgood toll station from its foundation.

Fifteen dairies operated at Lake Tahoe in the early 1870s. The basin's fertile meadows were conducive to summer grazing, and the industry provided products for the eastern Sierra well into the twentieth century. The meadows were also used for sheep pasturage beginning in the 1860s, to the detriment of the environment. The sheep left few grasses, and their hooves tore up the meadowlands. In order to expand the sheep's grazing areas, each fall fires were set that cleared away brush and induced plant growth for the following spring. Charles H. Shinn, who wrote the classic history *The Story of the Mine,* worked as a government inspector at the turn of the century and called evidence of injury done to young trees by grazing "simply overwhelming." Eventually, the damage forced the sheep from the area; in such a fragile environment, it was an unsustainable industry.

Another industry that could not be maintained was commercial fishing. In the 1860s it seemed the native fish were unlimited in number, but by 1880 the California Fish Commission was induced to plant one hundred thousand young whitefish as well as nonnative trout in Tahoe, its tributaries, and the Lower Truckee. Because the introduced fish had

Tahoe City and its pier, circa 1886. (Courtesy Special Collections, University of Nevada, Reno, Library)

a disappointing success rate, two hatcheries—one at Tahoe City, the other on the Truckee River—were established to experiment with additional species that could survive in the lake and high mountain streams. The Tahoe City hatchery is used today as part of the University of California–Davis Tahoe Environmental Research Center (TERC) and has an interpretive section open to the public.

The most controversial of the species planted by the commission was not planted in Lake Tahoe at all. The cannibalistic mackinaw had been proposed as a plant in 1895. The commission purchased sixty-five thousand of the Great Lakes fingerlings, but resort owners objected to the introduction of the voracious feeders that run to thirty pounds. Instead, the fry were packed on horseback into the lakes above Meeks Bay. Some years later cutthroat were becoming scarce on the southwest side of Tahoe, and some of those caught looked to have been attacked, with scars or pieces of tail missing. In 1920 a fisherman hooked a six-pounder that looked different from any local fish. He cut off its head and sent it to the University of California, which identified it as a Great Lakes mackinaw. The predatory trout had migrated down Meeks Creek and established themselves in Tahoe. They hastened the commercial fishing effects on the native population. Although the California legislature banned commercial fishing at the lake in 1917, it was too late. The native trout had become extinct.

The American impact on the lake and its environs would change as resources were depleted. Tourism, which began on a limited scale when the lake was discovered and became pronounced with worldwide increases in leisure time, was innocuous in its early stages. A half century later, it had grown to such an extent that it created a marked impact on the lake's natural balance.

Chapter Five

Resorting

$\mathcal{V}$isitors had been accommodated at various way stations from the time of the first American lake-valley settlers. As modes of travel improved, the mountain lake became more accessible.

One of the early hotels exceeded all others in scale: the Deans' Lake House, built in 1859 on the south shore. It was built of logs that a *Sacramento Daily Union* correspondent said "exceed any we ever saw put into a house," and hundreds of visitors could be fed and lodged in it. In August 1863 William Brewer recounted overhearing two teamsters who stood at the bar sharing whiskeys. The first commented that there were a good many people about. The second agreed. What, wondered the first, are they doing? Nothing, said the second. "Nothing at all?" asked the first. "Why, yes," said the second. "In the city we would call it bumming." The teamsters threw down their drinks and left to go to work. Although tourism at the lake had not yet been accepted, drinking and driving had.

Raconteur Ramsdale Buoy and his companions from San Francisco made their junket to Tahoe in the spring of 1866. They explored Echo Lake, sailed Tahoe on the *Edith Batty,* and stagecoached through Lake Valley. Atop Johnson Pass they considered a shortcut called Hawley Grade, after pioneer Asa Hawley, that switched back and forth as it plunged fifteen hundred feet to the valley floor. Narrow and exceedingly steep, it was a "sheer drop," in Buoy's words. One member of the group commented that if the stage turned over on the run down, you could not hold an inquest with a microscope. Buoy said that their stage driver did not bat an eye, while they huddled in the back of the vehicle afraid to look down. "Several long pulls from our bottle fortified us, and we took off down the mountain." Making it safely to the bottom, some of the party started back up on foot to see what they had come over, but, in that altitude, they did not get far, returning "puffing and blowing."

When the Central Pacific Railroad had been completed in the late 1860s, the use of freight wagons diminished, greatly affecting the Bonanza Road's way stations. The exceptions were those hostelries on the lake that profited primarily from tourism. After 1880, with the Comstock veins playing out and the lake's original industries leveling off, the business of attracting tourists became of primary importance to the lake's economy.

On the east shore the Glenbrook House, at the head of a meadow a half mile up the canyon from the bustle of the bay's logging operations, had, since the mid-1860s, catered to discriminating guests. Its billiards room, ten-pin alley, and hand-carved cherrywood bar bespoke a resort atmosphere. If there were any doubts that its accommodations were intended for the discriminating class, rates of three dollars a day erased them.

Shakespeare Rock, a featured attraction, towered above the resort. Mrs. J. A. Benton was sketching the mountains in 1862 and recognized the resemblance of the feature to a profile of the bard's head. While reporting that everyone had to see the rock, renowned Comstock journalist Dan DeQuille commented, "There is much in the position from which it is viewed, and not a little in the imaginative powers of the person viewing it."

Throughout the 1860s and 1870s Glenbrook hosted Comstock mine owners and their San Francisco partners famous for engaging in all-night high-stakes poker games. Former president U. S. Grant and

At the end of the nineteenth century, the Glenbrook House, also known as the Glenbrook Hotel, charged guests an extravagant three dollars a day. (Courtesy Special Collections, University of Nevada, Reno, Library)

his wife were among the distinguished guests in the late '70s. In 1880 Rutherford B. Hayes, the sitting president, visited, accompanied by Gen. William Tecumseh Sherman, Secretary of War Alexander Ramsey, and the rest of the presidential party.

When the south shore's original shoreline hotel, the Deans' Lake House, burned down in 1866, the property sold to Thomas Benton Rowland. He built a small hostelry, some clapboard cabins, and his primary attraction: a dance pavilion and saloon. His annual "crusher" became the social event of the Sierra. Everybody who was anybody in Virginia City, Carson City, and Placerville received an invitation. In 1870 three steamers ferried guests from around the lake, and the stage service utilized additional coaches to carry partyers up Kings Canyon and Clear Creek Grade over Spooner Summit. A Sacramento City quartet played, and festivities lasted from 8:00 P.M. to 6:00 A.M. That morning all still standing took steamer rides around the lake. One coach full of partyers from Carson got lost and missed the dance entirely, settling for a view of dawn on the lake from Luther Pass. One couple from the west slope came to the party and stayed a week to recuperate.

Rowland's ability to recognize what the people wanted and to organize enabled him to become a proficient politician. He served two terms as the first California assemblyman to simultaneously represent two counties, El Dorado and neighboring Alpine.

Before the Lake House became Rowland's, surveyors had labeled the basin's south end "Lake Valley" because of its expansive, flat aspect. Settlers later gave names to five distinct areas in the south. The property below Johnson Pass, encompassing what originally was Yank's Station, became known as "Meyers" when German immigrant George Henry Dudley Meyers purchased the land in 1873. Moving toward Nevada, the next district took its name from the original appellation and was designated "Tahoe Valley." In 1907 Almerin R. Sprague built a hotel in the vicinity of Rowland's old hostelry and used his shortened first name in its designation, the Al Tahoe Hotel. The community around it took the name "Al Tahoe" from his establishment. The next area had originally been an important site to the Washoe Indians. It was a trailhead for a major pathway south and east to Carson Valley and had a large number of grinding stones, evidence of centuries of Washoe summer homes. As early as 1888 the area was called "Bijou," meaning "gem" or "jewel" in French, probably named by French Canadian lumberjacks who worked in the area. The community that developed and overlapped the California and Nevada border was called simply "Stateline."

Across the lake, on the northwest shore, the Grand Central Hotel, formerly the Tahoe City Hotel, laid its claim to being the finest establishment between San Francisco and Virginia City. The opulent three-and-a-half-story inn—featuring fifty commodious suites and apartments, two dining rooms, and a dance salon—was so well known and so majestic in appearance that it neither needed nor had a sign to identify it.

Yank and Liddy Clement moved their famous Yank's Station from the Bonanza Road at the base of Johnson Pass to the lake's south shore in 1873. They built a three-story hotel fronting the lake, which when completed in 1875 featured a dance hall that Rowland might envy because it featured the era's sensation: springs beneath its floor. Yank commented that the flooring allowed folks to dance whether they knew how or not.

A tall, well-heeled newcomer visited Yank's in the summer of 1879, admiring the stand of virgin timber that surrounded it, the beach, and the lake. When he returned a year later he bought the property: one mile of shoreline and two thousand acres of old-growth forest stretching from the lake to glacier-formed Fallen Leaf Lake. The buyer was Elias J. "Lucky" Baldwin, called Lucky because of his dealings in mining stocks and real estate. His eighty-five-hundred-acre Rancho Santa Anita and Santa Anita Race Track—both named for his daughter; his forty-six-thousand-acre tract that later became the Los Angeles suburb of Baldwin Hills and parts of Arcadia, Pasadena, and Monrovia; the exclusive Baldwin Hotel and Baldwin Theater in San Francisco; as well as the Tahoe hotel were all evidence of his "luck." Fortune of a different sort was evinced by his four marriages, with a widely circulated rumor of a fifth, and numerous publicized sex scandals, two of which involved accusers attempting to shoot him.

Baldwin named the Tahoe hotel the Tallac House, for Mount Tallac, the 9,785-foot peak with the cross of snow that rises alongside Fallen Leaf Lake. The Tallac House catered to a "tony" crowd, with the fashionable young ladies bringing at least one trunk of dresses so they might change to add color to the afternoon and again for the evening prom-

Lucky Baldwin's Tallac House Casino, "the marvel of the century." (Courtesy Special Collections, University of Nevada, Reno, Library)

enade. Although a tall, striking Washoe Indian, Ben James, led hunting and pack trips from Tallac, the bitter irony of how things had changed for Tahoe's Native people is captured in E. B. Scott's seminal work *The Saga of Lake Tahoe.* Reporting on the hotel's fishing services, Scott wrote that they tallied the daily trout catch by the hundreds. He continued, "An uprising was narrowly averted, however, when friendly tribesmen from the nearby Washoe encampment were forbidden to spear and net trout in streams flowing to the lake." The anecdote ends without telling how violence was avoided.

By the turn of the century, Baldwin had constructed a new hotel with electric lights, "turning night into day," steam plant–supplied heat, fountains, well-tended gardens, and a string orchestra playing afternoons and evenings. Gambling was not outlawed in California until 1911, and Baldwin built a three-story casino fronting the lake. Advertised as "the marvel of the century," besides roulette, dice, and blackjack, it featured a stage for theatricals and ten thousand dollars' worth of French plate mirrors.

Rates were high at Baldwin's, illustrated by a popular tale: A bandit, upon learning that his intended prey had come from time spent at Tallac, apologized, pressed a silver dollar into his victim's hand, and sent him on his way.

Although Baldwin can be seen as simply another wealthy libertine pursuing personal desires as well as a vision for his clientele, his stance regarding the two thousand acres of forest he purchased also merits him a place in Tahoe's environmental history. "My land acquisition will save this vast forest from the beauty-destroying ax of the woodsman," he proclaimed, "so that the magnificent pines and cedars may be admired by generations to come." He kept his word, preserving a large swath of the last virgin forests on the lake's south shore.

In 1888 Lake Tahoe hosted three thousand visitors, most from the eastern United States, although some European travelers as well. They were coming to the West to see its natural wonders, especially Yosemite Valley. More and more included visits to Tahoe on their sightseeing trips to view the lake and what remained of its forests. The father of Sierra conservationist John Muir described a juniper with a four-foot diameter at Sugar Pine Point as "the largest and finest in the Sierra." In reflecting on the range's glaciated lakes, he wrote, "Lake Tahoe is the king of them all, not only in size, but in the surpassing beauty of its shores and waters."

Mark Twain, the LeConte brothers, and William Brewer were among earlier visitors whose writings touted Tahoe's natural beauty. In August 1883 poet John Vance Cheney issued a comment typical of the succeeding era in the magazine *Lippincott's:* "For nature pure and simple, for chaste beauty and native grandeur, one will hesitate before naming the rival of Lake Tahoe." The naturalists' and writers' accounts, together with resorts' advertising, were making the lake a summer destination.

The winter tourist business did not exist until it was invented in Truckee, a satellite to Lake Tahoe's economy. Beginning in 1872 ice production became its primary winter occupation. Thousands of tons of ice were harvested from Donner Lake and the Truckee River (Lake Tahoe's depth and constant motion keep it from freezing) and stored in icehouses. It cooled the sweltering depths of the Comstock mines and kept California fruit and vegetables fresh when shipped out of state. Packed in hay, it was sent cross-country in insulated railcars so patrons of New York's or New Orleans's grand hotels could enjoy drinks over pure Sierra ice.

Toward the turn of the century, with much of the area's timber gone and Comstock ore veins played out, Truckee needed a boost to its economy. In 1895 newsman, politician, and city father Charles F. McGlashan introduced the idea of winter sports. He organized boosters to build a 700-foot oval ice-skating rink, illuminated by twenty arc lamps, and, in downtown, a 175-foot toboggan run that began above a structure with 3-foot-thick walls covered with chicken wire. Hosing down the grotesque building each night formed a giant "ice palace." The Southern Pacific Railroad (which succeeded the Central Pacific in 1884) began running an excursion train, called the Snowball Special, from San Francisco to Truckee for the West's first ice carnivals.

In the summer seasons people rode the train to Truckee and the stagecoach from Truckee's train station to Tahoe City. In 1899 some six thousand tourists, many of them Californians, came to the lake. But the ride from Truckee was about to change: Glenbrook's Bliss family had decided to revolutionize travel and resorting at the lake.

Lumber baron Duane L. Bliss had charged the San Francisco Union Iron Works with constructing the 170-foot twin-screw steamer *Tahoe*. It was built in the ironworks' yard. Workers then disassembled it and shipped it in sections by rail to Reno and then to Carson. From there Bliss had it hauled to the lake for reassembly.

A heavy-duty lumber wagon using the combined pulling power of eighteen horses and mules dragged the *Tahoe*'s oversized boiler up Spooner Summit. The team also hauled the immense firebox and every other section of the disassembled steamship up the long grade to Glenbrook.

Once it was riveted back together, the *Tahoe*'s hull, divided into eight watertight compartments that made it virtually unsinkable, displaced 154 tons. It utilized a six-person crew and could accommodate two hundred passengers. Its twin steam engines produced a total of 1,200 horsepower. Its sitting rooms featured teak and mahogany appointments, primavera or Spanish cedar panels, and Brussels carpeting. Launched in 1896, it steamed about the lake for forty years before falling into disuse and finally being scuttled in more than four hundred feet of water off Glenbrook in 1940.

Ernest John Pomin served as captain of the *Tahoe*, piloting the Bliss-family boats for nearly forty-five years. He captained the *Meteor* for the previous twenty years, then the *Tahoe,* until his death, from a slip and

fall on the boat, in 1917. Pomin was part of a nautical family at the lake that included his relations Tahoe City founder William, for whom the small steamer *Mamie* was built in 1877; the *Tahoe's* engineer, Ernest H.; the steamship *Nevada's* captain, Joseph H.; and John Ernest, a commercial fisherman and guide. Robert Pomin still operated a cruise boat on the lake in the 1950s, and descendants of the family continue to live in the Tahoe City area in the present day.

Beginning in 1901 the *Tahoe* circled the lake daily in summers, making stops at ports of call to unload and load passengers, mail, and supplies. The trip that required a week in the 1860s took the *Tahoe* eight hours. The steamer was part of the Bliss family's master plan to create a major transport firm, open new logging areas on the west shore, and expand and modernize the use of Lake Tahoe as a resort center. In 1898 they formed the Lake Tahoe Railway and Transportation Company, moving their business center from their logging operation in Glenbrook across the lake to Tahoe City.

Duane L. Bliss's son William, a graduate of the Massachusetts Institute of Technology, surveyed a narrow-gauge railway route from the Southern Pacific's line at Truckee, along the Truckee River, to the lake. The Blisses moved their rolling stock and equipment, opening rail passage to Lake Tahoe. To maintain a regular graded ascent, the tracks crossed the meandering river five times in one mile and eight times on the sixteen-mile line. A trestle pier that ran out an eighth of a mile over the lake served as the line's terminus. An overwater company store, post office, and warehouse were located on the pier, and steamers moored there. Off a sidetrack, on a knoll above the lake, the Blisses built what would become an internationally famous hostelry, the Tahoe Tavern.

Designed by Duane's twenty-eight-year-old son, Walter Danforth Bliss, already a noted architect and engineer, the many-gabled hotel was situated in a grove of virgin timber that the younger Bliss took pains to preserve. Tahoe Tavern had all the amenities luxury hotels offered at the turn of the century, including a single phone line that could be difficult to access since all other subscribers between Truckee and Emerald Bay shared it. The hotel also had lighting powered by a steam-generated plant that provided electricity for fifteen hundred lights.

In the early days management encouraged its guests to dress for its numerous outdoor activities, even when taking meals. By the 1930s attire was dressier, with lunch and dinner requiring "city dresses," coats, and ties. One young woman remembered her family's keeping extra white coats at their cabin so unprepared male guests could go dancing at the

The internationally renowned Tahoe Tavern in 1911. (Courtesy Special Collections, University of Nevada, Reno, Library)

Tavern ballroom. The hotel also had a casino, theater, bowling alley, and outdoor swimming pool. Drinking moved to the upstairs rooms during Prohibition, along with, as late as the 1940s, portable slot machines that could be moved to safety when the sheriff called to say he would soon be making a raid.

Boats and launches accommodated any number: The company had purchased three other steamships, including one named *Tallac,* which was lengthened by twenty feet amidships and rechristened *Nevada.* The *Nevada* carried passengers and mail, leaving the dock at Tahoe Tavern at the same time as the *Tahoe,* circling the lake in the opposite direction. The two would pass each other at Glenbrook, each returning in the early evening. The hotel also had a fleet of fishing boats.

In 1911 Clarence W. Vernon, a member of the Tavern orchestra and later Tahoe City's general manager of public utilities, met his fiancée, Ethel, in Truckee after not having seen her for five months. They met at 7:00 P.M. and were married at 8:00. Two days later they engaged a double rowboat from Duane Bliss and rowed off on a honeymoon trip around Tahoe. Leaving on October 9, they returned three weeks later, on October 29, having circumnavigated the lake. They dined on fish they caught and ducks Clarence shot, bathed in the October water, and slept on sandy beaches or pine boughs. The concluding entry in Clarence's diary of the trip reads, "We have had a wonderful time and we are both sorry that it is over."

Besides boats, the Tavern rented horses or driving teams, and cars with chauffeurs were available for those wishing to go on outings. People could walk to picnic in nearby Paige Meadow, named after one of the Paige brothers, who, as the story went, was hung there for slitting the throat of a horse. As an aside, the tale mentioned he had also murdered the horse's rider.

William J. Thomas, who, when he worked for the North Pacific Coast Railroad in 1901, built the first California cab-forward locomotive—providing the best visibility for engineers on sharp curves—worked as the master mechanic for the Truckee-to-Tahoe City railroad line. During winter months he served as chief engineer on the steamer *Tahoe.* Thomas was popular with the railroad employees, having played a key role in getting them a raise from six to eight dollars a day while simultaneously reducing work hours from ten to eight. Another popular Bliss employee was Toy Yat. In an era of extreme racism against Chinese, Yat managed a bunkhouse and eatery that served the company's crew at the pier at Tahoe City. In his honor the café was named the Toy Yacht Club.

Will Rogers stayed at the Tahoe Tavern in the fall of 1930, shooting scenes for the folksy movie *Lightnin'*, based on Nevada's quickie-divorce business. *Lightnin'* was successful because of Rogers's popularity, even though the action of the film slowed to a crawl with his ad-libbed anecdotes.

Of the numerous movies filmed at Tahoe, the one most often associated with the lake is Nelson Eddy and Jeanette MacDonald's *Rose Marie*. In 1935 filming took place at Cascade Lake, Carnelian Bay, and the sandbar at the mouth of Emerald Bay, where crew members built a Canadian-like Indian village, with teepees and totem poles. Rumors at the time that the film's two stars could barely stand to work with one another may explain why MacDonald remained aloof as Eddy often joined locals at the Tahoe Inn bar in the evenings, after shooting. The movie featured a young James Stewart as an escaped convict and some one thousand Washoe and Paiute Indians, who were used in crowd scenes. Herb Obexer, original owner of the west shore's Obexer Marina, was miffed to find that his payment for assisting in making the movie was a script—until he found a check inside it for five thousand dollars.

The use of Tahoe as a backdrop for films was subject to the continuing battle over use of the lake's waters between Nevada and California. In June 1902 President Theodore Roosevelt had signed the Newlands Reclamation Act, named for Nevada senator Francis J. Newlands, to develop western resources. In accordance with the act, the U.S. Reclamation Service was established. Its administrators hoped to use Truckee River and Carson River waters to reclaim more than two hundred thousand acres of Nevada desert by creating small irrigated farms. The plan to make the lands "bloom like the rose" was at best overly optimistic, for not even the massive lake could produce the amounts of water necessary to sustain it. In a reversal of the A. W. Von Schmidt dispute of the 1870s, the U.S. government fought against California to use large quantities of the lake's water for Nevada.

Although the newly formed U.S. Reclamation Service entered into negotiations for the purchase of the dam at the lake's outlet, an eastern power-company syndicate secured possession. In 1908 the syndicate struck a deal to provide water for the federal project. The one-sided lifetime agreement made Tahoe a storage reservoir for the company, which provided electricity to Reno and other Nevada towns. Tahoe property owners feared that the lake level would leave homesites and resorts high and dry in the summer and flood them in the winter.

The compact not only threatened Tahoe's scenic beauty but later proved to violate the national conservation policy instituted by Roosevelt. A 1909 *San Francisco Examiner* headline provides an example of the bitterness the agreement engendered in California: "Secret Deal with U.S. Puts Tahoe in Syndicate's Clutch." An amiable but excitable resident, Chris Nielsen, lived on the west shore and had a boatyard for maintenance and storage that later became Sunnyside Marina. At one point, believing the dam was going to be blown up, he rallied friends. They devised a plan to moor someone in a boat by the dam, believing that would stop the effort. Instead, neighbor Elizabeth Schmiedell Fennelly recalled, "Everybody went over with shotguns. It was all very exciting. Chris used to get very excited about things."

Workers replace logs and dirt with cement at the oft-disputed Truckee River outlet dam, circa 1912. (Courtesy Special Collections, University of Nevada, Reno, Library)

A three-term U.S. congressman and Tahoe property owner, William Kent, who donated twenty-three acres of west-shore land for a public campground that now bears his name, enlisted the National Conservation Association to fight the Reclamation Service project. Kent wrote the bill that created the National Park Service. He donated Northern California redwood lands for what later became Muir Woods National Monument and land for Mount Tamalpais State Park. Kent and the conservation association, which counted among its members Harvard and Yale universities' presidents and other influential national figures, lobbied the federal government and the California legislature. In 1911 California prohibited transportation of any fresh water of the state into any other state "for use thereto."

In 1913 the Nevada state legislature passed its own act, ensuring that the courts would be involved in any decision. Wishing to turn infertile land into arable farms, Nevada gave its consent for the federal government to use the lake's water "in such manner and to such extent" as needed for its purposes. The Reclamation Service proposed using up to six vertical feet of lake water. In 1915 a condemnation suit filed by the federal government won control of the dam for the Reclamation Service, but allowed it only two vertical feet of water.

The government encountered difficulties when releasing water into the Truckee River canyon because the river would flood. The Lake Tahoe Railway ran through the canyon, and debris piled up at each of its bridges, impeding the water flow. The government offered one hundred thousand dollars to help move the tracks to higher ground. Bliss company officials insisted that would cover only one-fifth what it would cost and demanded one million dollars. The dispute involved flooding that hampered the Southern Pacific Railroad's main line to Reno as well, and litigation continued into the 1930s.

In 1926, with business faltering, William Bliss approached the Southern Pacific Railroad people, suggesting the company lease the railroad right-of-way from Truckee to the lake for a dollar a year. He would sign the rights over to them if they rehabilitated the line, converting it to standard gauge, and thereafter ran through service from its Oakland station to Tahoe City. Southern Pacific agreed. A company largely associ-

founded in 1892; the presidents, faculty, and alumni of the University of California and Stanford University; and the governor and other officials from Nevada. In April 1899 President William McKinley signed a decree that set aside 136,335 acres southwest of Lake Tahoe as a reserve (forest reserves were called national forests after March 1907). The proclamation included this statement: "Warning is hereby expressly given to all persons not to make settlement upon the tract of land reserved by this proclamation." The area included Glen Alpine, what is now Desolation Wilderness—east of the Crystal Range—and the long stretch of shoreline between Rubicon Point and Camp Richardson, excluding already privately owned property. The first federally protected land in Tahoe Basin is now among the most heavily visited wilderness areas in the United States.

While the forest reserve and a portion of the west shore maintained its original forest and wild aspect, other parts of the lake had to recover from the earlier devastation of clear-cutting. By the end of the century old-growth trees were almost completely limited to those of the early estates and resorts, or those on unworkable slopes and higher elevations, and this led to a problem with fires.

Fires could devastate mature forests, as in Mark Twain's account of his escaped campfire in *Roughing It* or the fire in September 1889 that witnesses reported raging across many miles at Emerald Bay, destroying "the finest park of tree growth in all that region." But much more common were fires in the old clear-cut areas. Fast-burning chaparral replaced the forests and combined with the logging slash left behind to increase the threat of high-intensity fires. In 1898 a fire close to Meyers, the old Yank's Station, swiftly swept up the nearby mountains, destroying the hillsides. A forest agent reported in 1902 that there were many small smoldering fires on the California side of the lake, "four to ten in one day's travel." In 1903 a fire near Bijou on the lake's south shore burned unchecked for more than three weeks.

Although nothing like the original Jeffrey and sugar pine, as early as 1903 dense new woodland, with trees ten to twenty feet high, was emerging. In that year Albert F. Porter, of the U.S. Bureau of Forestry, met with representatives of major businesses, utilities, the California Chamber of Commerce, and the Sierra Club, finding widespread support for expanding forest reserves, except among local businessmen. Three important figures supported expansion: D. L. Bliss, powerful Nevada senator William Stewart, and President Theodore Roosevelt. The president was in the midst of doubling the amount of land in federal forest reserves. Stewart had proposed that Congress create a national park at Tahoe, but the bill had died. A reserve garnered more support because it did not prohibit businesses, such as logging or grazing, from utilizing the land. In October 1905 President Roosevelt issued a proclamation expanding the Lake Tahoe reserve. The new boundaries included much of the California side of the basin, except properties close to the lake, which, like most of the Nevada side, were largely in private hands.

As the forest's second growth developed, roads became a concern at the lake. In 1906 a Tallac Hotel brochure admiringly portrayed Mrs. Joseph Chanslor, who had driven solo from Sacramento to the resort in her Simplex, a four-cylinder racing car with a chain drive. Her car had carried extra tires, gasoline, and water, for there were no service stations along the way, and she had worn a duster, goggles, and veils as necessary accoutrements on the narrow dirt roadway. Throughout the entire area people talked of the feat, for she had arrived in the incredible time of eight hours.

In 1903 a magazine named *Outing* had promoted the possibility of

rediscovering America by automobile. Although the federal government established the Office of Public Roads in 1905, it served essentially as an advisory body, providing few funds. It was not until 1916, stimulated by the idea of a national coast-to-coast highway, that the government established substantial assistance for a road system. Until then the states needed to build and maintain their own roads. California had created a State Bureau of Highways in 1895. Its first report spoke of the general condition of the roads as suffering from "generations of neglect." Among its statutes regarding necessary projects the bureau listed improvements to the Lake Tahoe Wagon Road. It took fifteen years before voters passed a bond to substantially effect change, but at that time eighteen million dollars was allotted to establish a highway system.

Because of its continuous use beginning in the Comstock mining days, the road between Placerville and Tahoe rated with the best in the state. Of particular note in the early part of the twentieth century was the Richardson daily auto stage to the Tallac House. The drivers included Marion and Tod Burgess, African American brothers whose father had owned a blacksmith shop on Bonanza Road. For many years the Burgesses drove the Pierce-Arrow stage car to the lake, a service known to be thoroughly reliable, prompt, and efficient.

A state highway proposal in 1911 followed the trail from Meyers past

In the early twentieth century much of Lake Tahoe's road system was primitive. (Courtesy Special Collections, University of Nevada, Reno, Library)

Tallac and Emerald Bay to McKinney's. (McKinney's was later sold and renamed Chambers' Landing after the new owner. The road from there, through Tahoe City, to Truckee would be added to the state route in 1915.) In 1911, as well, the Nevada legislature appropriated twenty thousand dollars for construction and repair of the roads, the work to be done by convict labor.

In 1913 California apportioned money for work around Emerald Bay, and the later completion of Nevada's east-shore roadway would mean motorists could circle the entire lake. But construction around Emerald Bay was a difficult feat. The road, modern-day Highway 89, needed to be blasted from a sheer granite wall. One boulder alone weighed an estimated one thousand pounds. It required fifty cases of dynamite to break it into four pieces, which crashed down the mountainside. The falling rock was a portent as, to the present day, the early-twentieth-century engineering is unable to hold the granite above it in place. Periodic rock slides continue to close the road. Still, at the time of its completion, it greatly improved Sacramento's 260-mile circuit famously known as "the wishbone automobile route," which ran from Sacramento over Donner Pass, around Tahoe's west shore, and back by way of Placerville.

In the early decades of the century women emerged as owners of large Tahoe properties. Nathan Gilmore's daughter, Susan, managed the thriving Glen Alpine Resort for many summers. Desolation Valley's sparkling Susie Lake, which features a stand of wind-twisted old-growth junipers, many with circumferences of twenty-five feet, is named for her.

The woman who bought the first parcel in the north shore's Tahoe Vista tract in 1911 was not so honored. In fact, because of her acquisition, other prospective buyers questioned what type of development the owners planned. The original purchaser, Cherry de St. Maurice, from Sacramento, reputedly owned the finest and most notorious "parlor house" on the Pacific Coast.

Of the estates developed by people of means in the 1920s, the most spectacular is Emerald Bay's "Vikingsholm." Lora J. Moore Knight bought the property for $250,000 in 1928 from the William H. Armstrong family, which had owned it for forty years and ran a resort there. Mrs. Knight's wealth came from her father's and her first husband's business earnings. The men, both deceased, had been corporate lawyers and partners who ended up with large interests in railroads, the Diamond Match Company, and National Biscuit, among other businesses.

Knight had previously designed and built houses in Wisconsin, Reno, Santa Barbara, and St. Louis, as well as one at Observatory Point at Tahoe. Inspired by the fjordlike setting of the bay, Knight hired her niece's husband, architect Lennart Palme, to build a Nordic castle. They traveled, with other family members, to Scandinavia, studying architecture and purchasing furnishings. Utilizing two hundred workmen, it took less than a year to build the thirty-eight-room castle she called Vikingsholm.

Mrs. Knight demanded that the structure, built at the head of the bay, not impair old-growth trees. Because of this requirement, the square U-shaped foundation turns away from the bay, encompassing cedar and pine that reach 180 feet overhead. Stones were quarried in the nearby mountains. Wood was hewn, carved, and painted by hand at the site. Because antiques could not be exported from Scandinavian countries, craftsmen fashioned intricate, brightly painted copies of Nordic heirlooms for the castle's furnishings. The mansion, which still contains most of its original furnishings, is now a feature of the California State Park System and is open for public tours in the summer months.

On the island in the bay Mrs. Knight had a teahouse constructed: a single-room chalet furnished with a table and four chairs. She and her guests would take tea there, having been rowed out to the site by a servant. Observers commented on the curious sight of the dowager and her guests lounging in the stern of the boat, their weight lifting the purposeful oarsman high above the water.

Mrs. Knight became renowned for her benevolence. She provided financing for innumerable young people in California and Nevada to pursue educational opportunities. She sponsored Christian Science churches, including the one at Tahoe's south shore. Reports said that she helped finance Lindbergh's *Spirit of St. Louis* transatlantic flight as well. E. B. Scott recounted that at her death, in 1945, Mrs. Knight left each of her numerous servants and employees one thousand dollars. Scott commented, "This was considered by many to be little enough recompense for loyalty over the years, as some of her retainers had been in her employ for more than forty years. Then it was discovered that her bequest stipulated: '$1,000 for each *year* of service.'"

At the head of Emerald Bay, Lora J. Moore Knight constructed a thirty-eight-room castle, and on the island a one-room teahouse. (Courtesy Special Collections, University of Nevada, Reno, Library)

Lucky Baldwin, at age fifty-one, had married eighteen-year-old Jennie Dexter, who gave birth to a daughter, Anita. Jennie Baldwin died at age twenty-one. A newspaper reported, "If ever Lucky Baldwin had a soft spot in his heart it was for his wife Jennie Dexter and his daughter Anita." At his death in 1909, he left some ten million dollars in property to Anita, an equal amount to an older daughter, and substantially less to the daughter from an undocumented marriage. Court challenges over the will tied up payment until 1915, by which time the Tallac House, part of the estate bequeathed to Anita, had burned down. Later, all but three of the other resort buildings were leveled and their materials sold cheaply for salvage.

Through complicated title dealings the property came into the possession of Lucky Baldwin's granddaughter Dextra Baldwin Winter. Dextra, seemingly like all Lucky's immediate relations, was the marrying kind and had three husbands. In 1921 and '22, while married to her first husband, Ardine Winter—one of the founders of the Richfield Oil Company—she built a great cedar-log home on the estate. It is patterned after an eastern European hunting lodge and, like Vikingsholm, is a large U-shaped building. Its wings, bedrooms for servants' quarters and guest rooms, are situated around a stone courtyard and wishing well and face away from the lake. Although referred to as the McGonagle estate, the surname of Dextra's last husband, in all likelihood James R. McGonagle never set foot in the place. In recent years the property, managed by the Forest Service, has housed the Tallac Historic Site Museum.

The Forest Service also manages the two lakefront estates adjoining McGonagle's on the east. The three together are referred to as the Tallac Historic Site. The villas are a remnant of an era of conspicuous consumption by San Francisco millionaires. These were their summer retreats. The Pope family estate was originally built in 1894 for banker George P. Tallant, for whom Tallant Lakes above Meeks Bay are named. Another banker, Lloyd Tevis, and his son William developed the property more fully, and it passed through their hands to the Popes in 1923. The Pope patriarch, shipping magnate George A. Pope, playing on his surname, called the estate "Vatican Lodge." The grounds include many outbuildings behind the main house. A waterfall and trout pond, created in 1902, were originally fed by water diverted from Taylor Creek. The creek, which is the only outlet from Fallen Leaf Lake and runs into Lake Tahoe, is named for Pope's wife, Edith Taylor Pope. At the pond a teahouse sits amid exotic imported pine trees.

The Popes cruised the lake in a fifty-six-foot twin-engine excursion boat, *The Sheik,* named for their friend Rudolph Valentino's breakout movie. To maintain the craft's meticulous finish, Pope provided rubber-soled sneakers for his guests. The decking's varnish lost importance in World War II when the Popes donated the boat to the U.S. Navy for use patrolling California's coast. At his father's death in 1942, son George A. Pope Jr. gained control of the estate and trucked ponies from the Bay Area so he and his friends could hold weekend polo matches.

The third of the Tallac site's villas, Valhalla, has a fireplace whose stonework fills its great room's twenty-foot-high east wall. Its French doors open to a wraparound porch and a large lawn that leads down to its boathouse. Valhalla was constructed in 1923 for Claire Heller and her investment broker husband, Walter. When they divorced in 1936, they maintained joint ownership. They used it on alternate weekends until Claire Heller sold it in 1955. The house itself and the boathouse now serve as venues for music and theater performances and other events. Equally as spectacular as the buildings of the Tallac Historic Site are the massive pines, protected from nineteenth-century loggers, that tower overhead.

Another estate surrounded by old-growth trees, including one that John Muir labeled the finest juniper specimen in the Sierra, is atop a rise facing the lake at Sugar Pine Point on the west shore. The Ehrman mansion, a stately three-story Queen Anne Victorian featuring substantial turrets at each end, was built from native pines and Meeks Bay granite. The second story has circular master bedrooms at each end, with six guest bedrooms and eight bathrooms in between. It was commissioned by Isaias W. Hellman, the president of Wells Fargo Bank, and designed by architect Walter Danforth Bliss in 1900, shortly after Bliss completed Tahoe Tavern. Hellman's descendants sold the mansion to California State Parks in 1965, and it now serves as a prime example of early-twentieth-century "summer lodge" opulence.

At Glenbrook, on the east shore, in the early 1930s William Bliss refused right-of-way to the highway department, which wanted to run the highway along the lakeshore. Bliss argued that too much of the natural shoreline had already been disturbed. His decision forced the road's construction some miles from the lake. When the highway was completed, in the mid-1930s, the lake's steamships became defunct, as trucks hauled the freight and cars hauled the passengers. The steamers joined the railroad, which also lost out to the automobile. Symbolic of the change, two of the legendary steamers were scuttled in the lake by William Bliss, determined to find a fitting resting place for them. In 1939, halfway between Tahoe City and Glenbrook, the *Meteor's* sea cocks were opened; it settled heavily in the water, heeled sharply to port, righted itself, and sank into the depths. In 1940, several miles off Glenbrook, the *Tahoe* joined it, its bow pointing almost straight up before it slipped beneath the lake's waters. In 1942 the railway from Truckee to the lake was torn up, the track used as scrap metal to help the war effort.

On a point on the east shore is Thunderbird Lodge, George Whittell's estate. In the 1930s, when many people were suffering from the market crash, Whittell bought more than forty thousand acres of Tahoe property from the Bliss family's Carson and Tahoe Lumber and Fluming Company and the Hobarts' lands. He paid about twelve dollars a foot for lakefront land and more than one million dollars in all. The deal was brokered by Norman Biltz, who, as a commission, was given property above the Incline that he developed into the forty-three-acre Incline Lake. Biltz, known as the "Duke of Nevada," hosted power brokers and celebrities at the lake, many of whom he convinced to invest in the state of Nevada.

In 1937 Whittell began building Thunderbird Lodge, designed by Frederick J. DeLongchamps, the most prominent Nevada architect of the era. Built in a stand of mixed conifer, the property has a panorama of the entire lake. All the estate's buildings are stone. They include a gatehouse, caretaker's cottage, cook and butler's house, admiral's house, boathouse, and card house. These last two are connected to the lodge by underground stone tunnels so the owner could move about unobserved.

The stonework was done by Washoe Indians who camped on the property for three building seasons. The Washoe masons were superb craftsmen. They used salmon-colored rock from Carson City for the

The *Meteor,* sunk in 1939, first crossed the lake sixty-three years earlier. (Courtesy Special Collections, University of Nevada, Reno, Library)

main house and a gray stone for the walkways and bridges from the vast excavations across the lake at the Agate Bay quarry. The house and its outbuildings are a legacy to the Washoe masons. Former executive director of the Thunderbird Lodge Phil Caterino called their work "remarkable in its blend of natural thinking—how pathways go around, not through objects, lending a sense of harmony to the land. The fountains have the look of being built by nature's hand." It is, he said, "an amazing synthesis of masonry design."

Later much of Whittell's grand estate would become Nevada parkland. The other large private properties dictated development booms, as they were sold to be subdivided, or preserved the area's singular characteristics when sold to public agencies. In their heyday the elegant manors, a manifestation of conspicuous consumption, had created an image of Tahoe as the "Saratoga of the Pacific": an oasis for the wealthy. That image was balanced by its growing number of everyday visitors and a history that included truly unique residents.

Chapter Seven

The Eccentrics

From its earliest days of American arrivals, Tahoe has hosted its share of distinctive personalities. In the nineteenth century there were storytellers like Yank Clement and Cock Eye Johnson, and Lucky Baldwin, his daughters, and granddaughter, all tying and untying the marriage knot time after time. There was also the "Hermit of Emerald Bay."

In 1863 Richard Barter, a former first mate in Britain's Mercantile Marine Service, took up residence in the wilds of Tahoe's western shore. Barter became known as the "Hermit of Emerald Bay," and there are few spots for a hermitage as spectacular. Poet and early-day visitor John Vance Cheney called Emerald Bay, with it varicolored water and small rock island rising 150 feet above the water, "the gem of the Tahoe Scenery."

Ben Holladay, the overland stagecoach magnate, and his son bought the land originally called Eagle Bay in the early 1860s and built the lake's first private villa. The two-story residence foreshadowed part of Tahoe's future, as people of wealth soon identified the lake as ideal for a fashionable summer address. The Holladays brought in Barter to serve as caretaker.

Living alone on the west shore, Barter survived several harrowing incidents. Once, while shoveling snow from his cottage roof, he watched an avalanche break loose at a summit three thousand feet above him.

He thought his time had come and merely dropped his shovel to watch as boulders, massive trees, earth, and snow roared at him. But an over-hanging ridge caused the tons of debris to skip over his head. He esti-mated that the rubble missed him by ten feet. As it crashed into the bay, water splashed hundreds of feet in the air. Another time he spent part of a winter night submerged in the lake, with only his nose exposed to the below-freezing air, after his boat capsized. Managing to somehow scull the half-sunken boat back to the bay, he lay in a stupor for days, eating only what he could reach from his bed. He nursed himself for several months, thereafter displaying for his infrequent visitors a box in which he kept the toes he had amputated.

Barter claimed that the amount of icy water in the Sierra would not allow temperance. *Tahoe* was the Indian word for beer, he said: "It's put down that-a-way in the dictionary. I seed it myself." He excavated a grave on the island and built a miniature Gothic chapel over it. On visits to the north and south shores he told saloon friends to bury him on the island

Before Vikingsholm, Emerald Bay formed the spectacular sur-roundings to Richard Barter's hermitage. This photo from the 1950s shows, on the mountain to the left of the island, the massive slide area that dates to Barter's time. (Courtesy Spe-cial Collections, Uni-versity of Nevada, Reno, Library)

if his body ever washed up on shore. On a stormy mid-October night in 1873, Barter attempted to sail home from a sociable evening at Pomin's Tahoe House. A squall swept his boat off course. The craft splintered on the rocks at Rubicon Point, where the water drops off to fourteen hundred feet. His plans for burial were undone because, as with fourteen others drowned in the lake before him, his body never surfaced.

Another peculiar nautical case involved Orsamus W. Dickey, married to Flora Rowland, daughter of Tom Rowland, the south-shore hosteler who represented two counties simultaneously in the California General Assembly. In the early 1890s Dickey rowed out on the lake for Glenbrook but never arrived. Neighbors assumed he had joined those whose bodies are never recovered after boating accidents. Perhaps it was a suicide, some conjectured.

It was not until five years later that an old acquaintance recognized a scruffy, bearded Orsamus in Alaska. The contact told Orsamus he "would know him anywhere." Dickey conceded defeat, saying, "Just might as well go on home to Tahoe now." The family welcomed him back, believing he had just needed a temporary change of scenery. When Orsamus and Flora had a houseboat dragged up onto the shore at Bijou, converting it into a house, others thought the act judicious: ensuring that he would not pull up anchor some night and disappear again.

In the twentieth century there were those at the lake who behaved in capricious or unconventional fashion as well. One example in the early 1900s: the well-educated but self-destructive 260-pound Martin Lowe. Adhering to hermit Barter's philosophy regarding intoxicants and the Sierra, Lowe generally stayed drunk. Except for an occasional brawl, he was a bosom friend to all mankind. Hardened and unflinching, he would dive between ice floes in the river or argue over fish prices while standing barefoot in the snow. When a meat hook skewered his hand, he treated it with whiskey, used externally and internally, until it healed over. He limped about with a twisted leg. It had been run over by a logging wagon, and when the doctor prepared to amputate, Lowe escaped through a window. Although he was a fisherman, in the century's first decade his main reliance for revenue came to be diving from McKinney's or the Homewood Resort's pier for coins. As tour boats arrived, he urged visitors to toss "color" into the water that he would retrieve, his preference being gold pieces.

The giant Lowe never failed to emerge with the valuable except once when he dove and missed the lake. Crashing nose first onto a steamer's guardrail, he toppled underwater and remained there. The throng that had seen him sink crowded along the railing. Locals ran to the pier. A young acquaintance who had rowed out to search alongside the ship eventually thought to check on the other side. There Lowe floated on his back, waiting. Before the youngster could yell to him, Lowe dove under the hull to surface where he had disappeared. The crowd roared, greeting him with a hero's welcome. How had he survived so many minutes underwater? It was a miracle. At the bar, as drink after drink was foisted upon him, he could only agree.

Whenever someone lost something in the lake, the locals called Lowe. So it was that one early evening when, as she stepped off a tour boat, a mistress known to be worth several million dollars dropped her gold mesh purse. Lowe appraised the situation and announced the hour too late and the lake too cold to retrieve it. Since neither darkness nor cold had ever stopped him before, some speculated that he was too inebriated, although that had never stopped him before, either. Regardless, he said retrieval would have to wait until morning.

McKinney's Resort pier where the giant Martin Lowe would dive for "color." (Courtesy Special Collections, University of Nevada, Reno, Library)

Folks spent the night at the bar wagering on the number of dives it would require to retrieve the purse. Even if Lowe was hungover, the first attempt seemed the best bet. Early the next morning the smart money won when he climbed atop a piling to dive deep and secure the bag for the woman. Both she and Lowe were speechless when she opened the clutch and found it empty. She had lost a considerable number of gold coins; he had lost his reward. When the woman left on the steamer, his friends were amazed to find Lowe, for the first and only time, buying rounds for the house, using gold coins.

Despite his ne'er-do-well ways, Lowe also exhibited heroic behavior, on three occasions rescuing individuals who were drowning. But as he aged, his dissolute lifestyle caught up with him. Dressing in a loincloth and moccasins, his hair and beard wild, he survived mostly on handouts.

A character who gave more than he received was Tahoe City's Bill Boyle, whose grave sits atop the mountain above town. Originally from Georgia, Boyle wandered into Tahoe City after the turn of the century, about the time Lowe was engaging folks on the west shore. Boyle was a fisherman, a big man with an affable personality. When he was not on the lake himself, he built fishing boats and sold them at cut-rate prices. He baked donuts and pies and hosted the town's children, and, somewhat uncommon among whites, he befriended the Washoe Indians who camped by the Truckee River outlet.

One day Boyle agreed to fill in as the bartender at the Custom House on the wharf. When Frank Campbell, the owner, arrived, the place was packed with joyous souls. Campbell elbowed his way to the bar, ecstatic at the business until he realized the absence of the cash register's familiar ring. When asked, Boyle quietly told the owner it was high time somebody gave a party for the boys, so he was dispensing drinks on the house. At the price of several cases of whiskey, Boyle made Campbell the most popular man in town.

Toward the end of his life, Boyle let it be known that he wanted to be buried out on Rubicon Point, but in February 1912, when he died, the weather would not allow it. Instead, a group of seventeen men, fortified at the pub, loaded him on a toboggan and pulled him up the snow-covered five-hundred-foot hill. It took about three hours, and the boys continued to fortify themselves by passing a whiskey bottle around as they climbed. E. J. Pomin reported that about halfway, the boys "were getting pretty well filled up." It began to look like they might not make it to the top of the mountain. When the bottle inexplicably disappeared, they were able to finish their task. They always wondered about the rest of that whiskey. Pomin never told them that when no one was looking, on Boyle's behalf, he had thrown it away.

For many years, more than just Boyle's grave stood above Tahoe City. Protecting the town from above the town's commons was a brass cannon. It was the possession of Glenbrook founder Augustus Pray, and his name remains fixed in Sierra lore mainly because of the gun, not the establishment of the site. When he came to Glenbrook, Pray brought the twelve-pound howitzer reputed to be the famous piece abandoned by Frémont in 1844. The Civil War had broken out when Pray acquired it, and he reportedly kept the cannon from falling into the hands of "belligerent adherents of the South." It went missing for a time after Pray's death until rediscovered on a scrap heap at Glenbrook and transported across the lake. At the turn of the century it sat above the commons. A wide array of entities attempted to gain possession of the piece through the years, and locals hid it in a variety of places to foil their attempts. In the end Will A. Bliss donated it to the Nevada State Museum in Carson City, where it is now generally known as the Pray Cannon. Interestingly, evidence based on the location where it was originally found indicates that the coveted gun never belonged to Frémont.

A time after Pray founded Glenbrook and before the cannon was moved to Tahoe City, internationally renowned surgeon Dr. Charles Brigham began buying property on the lake's southwest shore. By the 1890s his thirteen hundred acres of land included Cascade Lake and lakefront property from southeast Emerald Bay to Baldwin's Tallac estate. For two winters, in 1926 and 1927, a Stanford University student hired by Brigham's widow, Alice, worked as caretaker of the Brighams' four-bedroom house on the shore above Tahoe. Alice, her two daughters, and their families, including husbands and seven grandchildren, lived there summers. Perhaps because the caretaker was a Stanford student, the family treated him like one of them, allowing him to take meals with them and join them on outings. They were fond of him, although they thought him a little odd. In the winter the caretaker lived by himself

Cascade Lake, part of Dr. Charles and Alice Brigham's estate. (Courtesy Special Collections, University of Nevada, Reno, Library)

in an adjoining cabin. He wrote to a friend at Stanford that of the seven deadly sins, only gluttony and lust were worth pursuing; he intended to work them to the limit. He commented, "I wish I were a Catholic. It would be nice to tabulate my delinquencies before a priest."

Snowbound, the caretaker invented systems to increase efficiency. He had a line from a boathouse out in the water attached to a bell in his cottage so the steamer's captain could alert him when he arrived with mail and provisions. He practiced flicking a match into a hole atop his wood-burning stove until he perfected the technique. At night he placed a cup of kerosene at the hole and ran a string to his bed. Mornings, with temperatures around freezing, he could pull the string, tipping the kerosene into the stove, and flick a lighted match to ignite a fire before leaving bed.

The caretaker never amounted to much as a student, never graduating from college. But he wanted to be a writer and constantly read books from the Brighams' extensive library. In the summer the Brighams would find teacups and glasses around the woods where he absentmindedly left them after reading or writing outdoors. Absentmindedness is not the best characteristic in a caretaker, as the Brighams discovered during that first winter. In December a hazardous tree near the house fell, and a limb crashed through the roof. Cutting down the trees around the house had been on the caretaker's to-do list. It continues to be important that snow is shoveled from roofs to eliminate the possibility of cave-ins. Unfortunately, the second winter a sudden heavy snowfall caused an even larger portion of the Brighams' roof to collapse. Luckily, John Steinbeck's limitations as a caretaker did not negatively affect his literary career.

While Steinbeck was becoming famous despite eccentricities, George Whittell Jr. was illustrating how immense wealth can allow one to nurture them. Moreover, because of his unconventionality, thousands of acres in the Lake Tahoe Basin were protected from development, including some twenty-four miles of shoreline. Whittell was born into wealth, as grandfathers on both sides of his family made millions taking advantage of Gold Rush lending and real estate opportunities. His father, a cutthroat business manager, added to the fortune.

Time and again his parents were disappointed by young Whittell, who followed whims rather than their advice. He was the real-life boy who ran away to join the circus. Instead of going to college as his parents wished, he joined Barnum and Bailey. He used his allowance to finance trips to Africa with the renowned Frank Buck, known as "Bring 'Em Back Alive Buck," to capture wild animals. Rather than taking part in an arranged marriage to a socialite, Whittell eloped with a chorus girl. When that marriage was annulled, he married Josie Cunningham, a member of the Florida Sextet stage group. The couple soon divorced, and Cunningham went on to appear in more than sixty movies.

Whittell's daring nature brought him fame as well. In San Francisco's 1906 earthquake, at age twenty-four, he used one of the few automobiles available to save family and friends. After attending several colleges in Europe, and becoming fluent in seven languages, he served in World War I, driving ambulances for Italy and France. When the United States entered the conflict, he joined its ambulance service. He suffered a wound and received decorations from the Allied governments for valor under fire. While recuperating, he fell in love with his nurse, Elia Pascal. Finally gaining his parents' approval of a relationship, Whittell married Elia in 1919.

When George Sr. died in 1922, he left his son some thirty million dollars. In the 1920s the younger Whittell shrewdly managed his investments, nearly doubling his inheritance. In 1929 he made his smartest move by cashing in fifty million dollars in stocks before the market crash—perhaps helping precipitate it.

One building on Whittell's Lake Tahoe property not mentioned before is an elephant house. Whittell had a lifelong love of wild animals, keeping a zoo at his home in Woodside in the Bay Area. When he summered at the lake he brought at least two animals with him. Mingo, his pet baby elephant, did not get much use out of the special house built for him. He got sick at the lake and had to be returned to Woodside. Always accompanying Whittell to the estate was his favorite pet, a lion named Bill that he raised from a cub. On occasion, when Whittell drove around town, Bill might be seen sitting in the passenger side of the convertible's front seat, paws on the dash, mane blowing in the wind. At least once Bill joined his owner at the bar of a saloon.

Whittell originally intended to build casinos at Zephyr Cove and Sand Harbor and luxury-home tracts on other acreage. However, after building Thunderbird, he decided to keep the entire property for himself. As he aged he became more reclusive. His wife, Elia, preferred Paris with friends to Tahoe with her husband. He sometimes hosted all-night poker or drinking parties at Thunderbird, and guests included Howard Hughes and Baseball Hall of Famer Ty Cobb. There were rumors of his use of opium and unsubstantiated stories of nudes jumping from rock to rock and packs of German shepherds roaming the grounds. What is known to be true is that he spent much of each summer on his secluded property alone with his secretary-mistress and his exotic animals.

If boats wandered too close to Thunderbird, they tripped an alarm that set off flashing spotlights, a strident siren, and the line from the Louis Armstrong recording of "Goody, Goody," blaring, "I'll be glad when you're dead, you rascal you!" Realizing the potential inherent in such a setup, teenagers from Crystal Bay built a raft with a flagpole and pushed it over the water to trip the alarm. They then watched the fireworks as the armed and dangerous Whittell charged out to the grounds to stifle the impending invasion.

Whittell's own boat, also named the *Thunderbird,* was as glamorous

The teahouse at George Whittell's Thunderbird Lodge. (Courtesy Special Collections, University of Nevada, Reno, Library)

and unusual as his home. It was designed and built by naval architect John Hacker, who, among other craft, designed one of the PT boats. Whittell launched the *Thunderbird* in 1940. Quadruple mahogany planked, with a copper-sheathed underside, it is fifty-six feet long and features a series of teardrop stainless-steel cabins. It cost a reported $87,500. Rarely seen on the lake, his boat caused the same kind of wonderment and rumors as the lifestyle of its owner. It is now displayed at significant events on the lake.

Whittell donated a large forest above Carson City to the public and at his death, in 1969, left a considerable part of his fortune to animal rights' groups. His Lake Tahoe property was another matter. In 1958 the state of Nevada reached an agreement with Whittell that gave it use of a nine-acre stretch of beach. Named Sand Harbor, it became the first state park on Nevada's shoreline.

In July 1961 Nevada governor Grant Sawyer toured the basin. Amazed that so little of it allowed public access, he urged the state legislature to open negotiations with Whittell. There were various unsuccessful efforts and a promising bistate bill that would have allowed California to help finance the project. To Sawyer's bitter disappointment, after heated debate, the joint proposal died in committee in Nevada. Finally, in 1966, when further negotiations to buy Sand Harbor and other parts of Whittell's land broke down, the state initiated condemnation proceedings. Because of the animosity that developed, Whittell allowed the sale of the Incline to private developers, who created Incline Village. Private investors were also competing for other of his lands in 1967 when a jury verdict found for the state. Some five thousand acres, including Sand Harbor State Park, were acquired for three million dollars. Other lands were added later, until the Nevada State Park at Lake Tahoe included roughly thirteen thousand acres.

Whittell's poker partner, the baseball all-time superstar and eccentric Ty Cobb, also maintained a house at Tahoe. Playing in the first decades of the twentieth century, Cobb was the first player enshrined in the Baseball Hall of Fame. He is generally acclaimed as one of the top three or

The fifty-six-foot quadruple-mahogany-planked *Thunderbird* motorboat. (Courtesy Special Collections, University of Nevada, Reno, Library)

four players of all time. The epitome of a fiery competitor, he spiked basemen, cursed umpires, and brawled with opponents and teammates alike. A teammate from the Detroit Tigers, who requested anonymity, told renowned sportswriter and Cobb biographer Al Stump, "A few of us who really knew him well realized that he was wrong in the head—unbalanced. He played like a demon and had everybody hating him because he was a demon. That's how he set all those records that nobody has come close to since 1928." Cobb used some of his multimillion-dollar fortune to endow a hospital for the poor in his hometown of Royston, Georgia, and he set up an educational foundation that helped hundreds of needy students through college. But when fans wrote asking for his autograph, he used the stamps from return envelopes for his own mail and burned the letters, saying it saved on firewood. Two wives, several mistresses, butlers, housekeepers, chauffeurs, nurses, and friends were driven off by the combative former star's ego and wild temper. At seventy-three, a miserly old man, he lived part of the year alone in his Tahoe hideaway—a ten-room lakefront hunting lodge.

When sportswriter Stump came to record Cobb's memoirs, the former Tiger teammate and a Cobb in-law tried to warn him off. Still, Stump wondered, how fanatical could the old man be? He soon found out. When he arrived Cobb was taking numerous medicines for an unending assortment of ailments. Because doctors had told him to stop drinking whiskey, he now drank a quart a day. Stump stayed with the ballplayer for several months. Cobb's continual outbursts of temper included throwing things and shooting off a Luger that he kept with him at all times, sleeping with it under his pillow. Tantrums caused the writer to have to pull Cobb out of saloons, motels, and casinos.

In the early-morning hours one midwinter night, with deepening snow on Highway 50 requiring chains and the highway patrol warning drivers to avoid it, Cobb insisted on going to Reno to gamble. When Stump tried to talk him out of it, Cobb exploded, "Don't argue with me! There are fee-simple sonsofbitches all over the country who've tried it and wish they hadn't."

There were two cars: Cobb ordered Stump to drive the one with chains; the former ballplayer would follow his tracks in an Imperial limousine, without chains. Sick, drunk, and with poor eyesight, Cobb made it to the summit, where the cars encountered a whiteout. As Stump crept along, his head out the window to gain visibility, Cobb laid on the horn. When Stump refused to go faster, Cobb finally sped fishtailing past. Several miles farther, near a curve, Cobb's limousine ended up nose first in a snowbank. Twenty yards away a two-hundred-foot cliff fell away from the road. "Bumped my—head," he said, and cursed the highway department for not lighting the spot. Drinking scotch from a thermos, he insisted they continue to Reno. At dawn they arrived, and Cobb played craps until getting thrown out of the casino for attacking a croupier whom he accused of touching the dice.

Cobb left Tahoe for the last time when, after he passed out, a doctor made a house call and announced that the Hall of Famer had to go to the hospital. Cobb had no intention of following the advice; he told the doctor to just send the bill. One of the last times Cobb talked to Stump, he said, "I had to fight all my life to survive. They were all against me. . . . But I beat the bastards and left them in the ditch. Make sure the book says that." He died a short time later. From all of baseball, only three men attended the funeral.

Although some of the eccentric characters were self-destructive, they did no damage to the lake's environment. In fact, by keeping their outsized properties mostly for themselves, Lucky Baldwin and George Whittell can be viewed as effective stewards of the land. Other developments at the lake in the first half of the twentieth century were small enough to limit any harm they might cause. But some evolved into grand projects that turned out to be as destructive to the health of the lake as the clear-cutting of its forests in the nineteenth century.

Chapter Eight

Developments

*A*t the turn of the twentieth century visionaries looked past the Tahoe region's denuded landscape to what the area might again become. In 1899 Gifford Pinchot, later the chief forester for the United States, lobbied the federal government to buy logged-over areas of land that could reproduce forests. Late that same year Nevada senator William M. Stewart initiated a proposal that the entire Lake Tahoe Basin be made into a national park. Civil engineer and conservationist Marsden Manson took a different approach, urging that the area be made a forest reserve. A reserve would protect the watershed but allow local uses such as logging and grazing. None of the ideas gained approval. Periodically thereafter, bills promoting the idea of federalization to protect the lake's environs were introduced in Congress but failed.

Five county governments share jurisdiction in the basin with the states, California and Nevada. The fragmented authority has caused continuous problems; without integrated government protection, the area evolved with various regulations and varying results in the diverse locales around the lake. The lake became one of the country's premier destination resorts and suffered the ill effects of urbanization. Its growth was due in part to the changing face of America.

Beginning after the Depression, and escalating dramatically at the end of World War II, a burgeoning middle class took to the roads. Taxes were used to improve highways and purchase parklands. At the same time,

Tahoe boosters and entrepreneurs publicized the lake's natural attractions and created new ones that advanced the area's economy. Camping, hiking, and fishing were augmented by boating, skiing, and recreational summer sports. Nevada, needing to expand its economic foundation beyond ranching and mining, sought to draw tourists by legalizing gambling and liberalizing its laws regarding divorce.

In the 1920s, with the mass-produced automobile increasingly affordable, car camping, or "gypsying," had become popular as a simple, inexpensive way to vacation. In 1929 an estimated 1.88 million cars took to the road in California. As highways were improved, camping escalated and so did problems associated with it, including garbage disposal, stream pollution, and trespassing. Campgrounds and tourist courts, the forerunners of motels, solved some of the difficulties.

By 1925 roadways completely encircled the lake, and vacationers began finding their way over California highways. Tahoe had only one state park, a heavily used campground near Tahoe City that originally served as the fish hatchery, so facilities were developed to cater to the motorists. Meeks Bay Resort on the west shore, Camp Richardson to the south, Globin's in Al Tahoe, Conolley's and Young's resorts in Bijou, and Zephyr Cove Resort on the east shore all offered rustic cabins as well as tent platforms and campsites. Each maintained a general store and offered rowboats and other amenities.

At the end of the decade the Bliss family offered to donate half of a nine-hundred-acre parcel of land on the west shore to the California State Park System if a proposed California bond issue to buy parkland gained voter approval. The property, near Emerald Bay, included nearly fifteen thousand feet of lakeshore and was valued at $265,000. When the bond issue passed overwhelmingly, the Bliss property became the first project on which its funds were expended. After four years of negotiation, the parties completed the deal, creating D. L. Bliss State Park.

As in California, the early Tahoe roadways on the east shore were graded but otherwise unimproved gravel roads. In the late 1920s the Nevada Highway Department and the Bureau of Public Roads began improvements. The Forest Service highway-funds program allotted $245,833 to the State of Nevada in January 1931. The money was used to construct a highway around the Nevada side of the lake. A Department of Highways publication noted, "The completion of this thoroughly modern and beautifully scenic highway along the rim of Lake Tahoe will increase tourist travel to Lake Tahoe and adjacent points in Nevada to a marked extent."

Just as with the Bonanza Road in the 1860s, the main obstacle to the roadway was the Washoe Indians' sacred site, Cave Rock. Rather than improving the trail behind the majestic landmark or the trestle bridge over the lake, planners designated $86,000 for construction of a 151-foot tunnel and a "two lane auto road" through it. No one consulted the Washoes, or even notified them, regarding the proposed tunnel. The white people, as a rule in that era, did not talk to the Washoe people. At the tunnel site, heavy cables were swung down over the rock face in preparation for the drilling, and in June 1931 construction crews moved their machinery and materials into place. The work, less regimented than that of today, followed a procedure described in one report as "drill, load, tamp, set the charge and then run like hell." Washoes in Carson Valley later recounted the shock they felt when the blasts occurred. By October the crews finished the tunnel, and in 1934 they completed the entire highway, "state line to state line."

At Squaw Valley, on the other side of the lake, in the early 1930s Wayne Poulsen fished and hiked with a friend whose father had at one time herded sheep there. When he graduated from the University of Nevada in 1938, Poulsen leased land and opened Nevada's first ski area at Mount Rose, northeast of the lake. His slope offered a ski school and consisted of a warming hut, heated by a potbellied stove, and a gasoline-

An auto barge, circa 1920, used rather than circling the lake on unimproved gravel roads. (Courtesy Special Collections, University of Nevada, Reno, Library)

operated 560-foot rope tow. When Poulsen's lease ran out, the landowner would not renew it, as he thought to try his own hand at running the ski area. So, while on leave from military service in World War II, Poulsen turned his sights to Squaw Valley and began buying land from Southern Pacific.

Completely encompassed by mountains, Squaw Valley adjoins the Truckee River Canyon not far from the river's headwaters at Tahoe City. Its proximity to the lake generally ensures its inclusion in histories of Tahoe, even though it is not technically part of the Tahoe Basin. By the mid-1940s Poulsen had decided to develop a destination ski resort by creating runs above the valley.

Another of Tahoe's ski-industry pioneers, Bill Klein, arrived in the area in the summer of 1936. Klein and his brother Fred were brought from Austria to start a ski school just outside the basin at Donner Pass. They had been invited by Dr. Joel Hildebrand, the manager of the U.S. Olympic Alpine Team and president of the Sierra Club. Hildebrand wanted to start a ski school near the club's Clair Tappaan Lodge. The brothers hiked to the top of a summit and looked down on Donner Lake. Seeing nothing but granite boulders, they wondered where people might ski. Hildebrand assured them that in winter, snow would blanket everything. The brothers stayed, and when the snow came they began teaching. Lessons consisted of everyone trudging up Mount Lincoln, skiing down, and doing it again.

In World War II, Klein, like several other experts from the area, trained the army's Tenth Mountain Division skiers. After the war he returned to become one of the premier figures in the area's ski scene. He became director of the ski school at Donner Summit's Sugar Bowl, which had opened the first chairlift in the Sierra Nevada in 1939. Klein helped found the California Ski Instructors Association and, owing to his prolific career, earned the Lifetime Achievement Award from the Professional Ski Instructors of America.

Others who were prominent in developing the lake's ski resources included Harvard Business School graduate Peter Klaussen, who built the Alpine Meadows Ski Area from scratch, walking the area's open bowls and deciding which trees needed to be removed and the placement of lift towers. Another Austrian, legendary instructor Luggi Foeger, designed Ski Incline. Foeger could be demanding on the slopes. He evaluated one group of aspiring instructors as having skied like "pigs, absolutely like pigs." After work he would clown, wearing a wig to a social gathering or putting onion rings over his ears at a dinner party.

Outdoor athletic endeavors were also a large part of summers at the lake in the 1930s and 1940s. The Glenbrook tennis courts hosted champion Helen Wills Moody, and its golf course hosted celebrities and professionals, including Hall of Famer Ben Hogan. The caddies were equally impressive. Among those who carried bags were Robert Davenport, who later served as clerk of the Nevada Supreme Court; Richard Jepson, who in World War II served on the *Enola Gay*, the plane that dropped the first atomic bomb; and the four Laxalt brothers, sons of Basque immigrants. Two of the brothers became successful lawyers, Paul Laxalt became Nevada's governor and served as a U.S. senator, and Robert Laxalt, writing about the Basque experience, became perhaps the most distinguished author in Nevada history.

In the late 1930s, at Glenbrook, Will Bliss and Rodeo Cowboy Association roper Johnny Vance, who managed the stables, built a roping arena with three rows of bleachers. They invited cowboys from western Nevada ranches and held calf-roping and team-roping events. Three Sundays each summer, year after year, eighty to one hundred competitors would participate after the grand opening, which featured a scratchy 78-RPM recording of the "The Star-Spangled Banner" resounding off Shakespeare Rock.

Although legalizing gambling in March 1931 increased Nevada's economic potential, it produced little revenue for the state in the '30s. At the lake the exception was the Cal Neva Casino at Crystal Bay. When its original building burned down in May 1937, it had been doing so well that construction workers were employed around the clock, and they rebuilt it in thirty days. At the same time, on a finger of land that extended into the lake, the beautifully appointed Ta-Neva-Ho, later the Crystal Bay Club, hosted patrons at casino games and nine slot machines.

During World War II, owing to gas rationing as well as the nation's patriotic fervor, Tahoe fell silent. Basin inhabitants included only caretakers at a handful of sites around the lake and an occasional tourist. Skiing and other winter recreations were suspended, and buildings

were shuttered. Snowplowing took place only on Highway 40 (which ran roughly parallel to modern I-80), considered essential for defense purposes.

In the war-depressed summer of 1942, a group of Sacramento businessmen, including renowned restaurateur Frank Fat, purchased the Ta-Neva-Ho and seven businesses around it. Three years earlier Fat, a Chinese immigrant with a genial personality, had bought a restaurant near the California State Capitol that came to be dubbed the legislature's "Third House." In 1941 Fat and his family had stayed the night at a cabin in Bijou, only to be told the next morning they must leave, as Asians were not welcome. He turned the tables by buying into the north-shore business, and later the nearby Cal Vada Lodge restaurant as well. His Tahoe restaurants were successful, even as other parts of the establishments changed ownership. His Sacramento restaurant business expanded to second and third sites, and today his family's eateries are found in locales throughout California.

On the south shore the Stateline Country Club offered games of chance, but it was not much more than a soda fountain with a little gambling in the back. Next door was the Nevada Club, a log cabin that also hosted gaming.

Two developments in Reno set the stage for the immense success of casinos at the lake. In 1936 Harold Smith opened a club and began publicizing it by identifying it with western history. Its signs, featuring a cartoon illustration of a covered wagon with "Harolds Club or Bust" on its side, helped negate the stigma of casino activity, which until then was often identified with a hoodlum element or the underworld. When World War II ended, five thousand people a day visited Harolds Club. William Harrah's involvement in gambling was the other key factor in the creation of the large Tahoe casinos. He opened a bingo parlor, called the Tango Club, in Reno in 1939. From a few slot machines, a crap table, and a blackjack table, he quickly expanded, opening Reno's Harrah's Club in 1946, helping establish northern Nevada as a gambling center. By the end of the 1940s, even with Harrah as a competitor, Harolds Club attracted twenty thousand visitors a day.

At the south shore of the lake, in 1944, Harvey and Llewellyn Gross, formerly owners of a Sacramento meat-retailing business, opened another modest casino at Stateline. Across the street from the Stateline Country Club, it offered guests gaming at three slot machines and two blackjack tables, meals at a six-stool lunch counter, and twenty-four-hour gasoline. The Grosses followed Harolds Club's lead, using a western theme, calling their casino Harvey's Wagon Wheel and using a wagon wheel and longhorn skull for its logo. The Grosses were true partners, and in the early years they worked long days, taking turns preparing food, dealing cards, and pumping gas. In the 1950s, spurred by Llewellyn's enterprise, they expanded, until the Wagon Wheel filled an entire city block. In 1955, Bill Harrah, seeing the Grosses' success, created his own Tahoe casino.

In 1931, the same year Nevada legalized gambling, it reduced its residency requirement for divorce to six weeks. With divorces difficult to obtain in most states, the change solidified the state's reputation as a "divorce haven." Celebrities were among those who spent six weeks at the lake to gain legitimacy. In 1951 Rita Hayworth and Clark Gable each stayed at Glenbrook to establish residency. That fall the actress and director Ida Lupino stayed at the same Glenbrook house Hayworth had rented. She was carrying actor Howard Duff's baby. Duff, at the time radio's Sam Spade, visited her periodically, and the day after her divorce, they were married. Because of complications, Gable, staying at the Glenbrook Inn, remained at the resort into December, long after it closed. Everyone at the inn, workers as well as management, was struck by his everyman's charm as he helped the maintenance crew close up cottages and took meals with the employees.

As various elements attracted more and more visitors, Tahoe's infrastructure came under mounting stress. In 1950 Lester Nagy believed the lone pump truck at the south shore charged too much for its septic and cesspool service. He bought his own pump truck and ran the first out of business. As the only pumper in the area, he wondered why certain of the large resorts never needed his service. "I knew they had to pump," he said, "and if they didn't call me then who the hell are they calling?" His investigation revealed they were not calling anyone. They were doing their own pumping at night into Tahoe's tributaries or down to the lake itself. "They done it in an area that was secluded and they done it in an area where they owned a hell of a big chunk of land," said Nagy, "and nobody could detect it, but I did."

Nagy organized a group to petition El Dorado County for an election to form a utility district. The large resorts were not interested, and they wielded the power. When a hearing was called at the county courthouse, the opponents to the district were there in force with their attorneys. Nagy spoke before anyone else had a chance. He explained that resort owners had no need to be in attendance: "I don't know what these people are doing here. None of them are included in the district." The proponents had quietly drawn the district in discontinuous fashion to include only those who favored it; the opposition's properties had been excluded. The voters in the election, held in September 1950, approved the district by a vote of seventy-nine to fourteen. Many years later Nagy laughed that the "no" votes puzzled him, since he had "looked at every ballot that went in the box." After several years filled with missteps and false starts, the district built its small sewer system.

As Nagy thought would happen, once sewage was diverted from the downtown area, others decided to hook up "and not worry about their sewer running over in the backyard and stink like hell all over the place." Nevada's Douglas County Sanitation Improvement District formed shortly thereafter, and signed an agreement to pump sewage into the new system. One of the most important wastewater programs in the world had been initiated. With unrivaled demands for purity, it adapted technology from many industries and became the first wastewater treatment program to produce great volumes of highly reclaimed water to be reused. By the 1970s the treated water was being piped out of the basin, protecting Lake Tahoe and irrigating the Carson Valley. Nagy went on to own the local bowling alley, serve on the city council, and later become an officer in two area banks. In 1978 the North Tahoe Public Utility District mirrored the south shore's policy, piping sewage effluent to a treatment facility outside the basin.

Harvey West, a Placerville lumberman, made his own contribution to protecting the lake. West had operated a mill at Tahoe Valley during World War II. He owned 177 acres at Emerald Bay, including Vikingsholm, that he wished to sell. The California State Park Commission expressed its eagerness to buy the land but needed to find matching funds. Over the objections of the El Dorado County Chamber of Commerce, which wanted the land to remain available for private development so it would remain on the county's tax roles, West agreed to keep the property off the market. He then donated half its value to the state, which purchased the balance for $150,000. By 1954 the state had also secured the adjoining lands, creating a spectacular park, contiguous with Bliss State Park.

While the lake's parklands were being expanded, so too was another attraction, gambling. Two small, short-lived casinos, Tony's and Dopey Norman's, opened at Stateline, on the south shore, in 1953. These were snapped up two years later by Bill Harrah, whose Reno casino had grossed more than $1 million a year, beginning in 1948. He later sold the Tony's and Dopey Norman's properties to the Grosses, who would use them for their Harvey's property's expansion. The price was $5.25 million in cash, the most expensive casino purchase ever. Harrah then bought the Nevada Club and Stateline Country Club across the street and never looked back.

Harrah's original Tahoe operation consisted of a Quonset hut with a false front. Four years later the new Harrah's Tahoe replaced Harolds Club as what at the time was the world's largest single structure devoted to gambling. It included ten acres of parking and the "South Shore

In the mid-1950s William Harrah bought up several of these Stateline, Nevada, properties and began his Tahoe casino operations. (Courtesy Special Collections, University of Nevada, Reno, Library)

Room," an 850-seat theater and restaurant. Following the lead of Las Vegas and Reno, the Tahoe establishments were hiring big-name entertainment with a view to luring gamblers to their tables.

With tourism increasing exponentially, Harvey's expanded its operations. While changing the name from the Wagon Wheel to Harvey's Resort and Casino, the Grosses maintained their family orientation. On slow nights Harvey and Llewellyn could be found eating popcorn and sharing stories with friends and employees around the casino fireplace.

Back in 1931, when Nevada legalized gambling, it had left the control of operations to county and local officials. Although the state imposed stricter statewide measures in 1945, it was too late. The Cal Neva already had gangland figures as owners, including Elmer "Bones" Remmer, prominent in San Francisco's underworld, and Bert "Wingy" Grober, whose East Coast speakeasies were reportedly supplied by Joseph Kennedy's bootlegging operation during Prohibition.

Soon after Las Vegas mobster "Bugsy" Siegel's gangland-style murder in Beverly Hills in 1947, a man identified as Louis Strauss shot Harry Sherwood, owner of the Tahoe Village Resort at Tahoe's south shore, in Sherwood's own place. Sherwood had been associated with illegal gaming and bootlegging in the East, owned the gambling ship, *Lux*, which operated off the Southern California coast, and had done time in a federal prison for robbery. Strauss turned out to be an infamous gangster, "Russian Louie." When Sherwood died of complications from his wound, Strauss faced murder charges, but the jury acquitted him on grounds of self-defense.

As a young reporter, Nevada author Robert Laxalt had interviewed Strauss in the Carson City Jail. Laxalt described him as "a tall, thin man with a long face and dead eyes, but he was affable enough." The killer confirmed that he was indeed Russian Louie and readily admitted his gangland affiliations. Sometime later Strauss was picked up by two friends for a drive from Las Vegas to Los Angeles. Laxalt reported, "Russian Louie departed, but he did not arrive. . . . Rumor had it that he was 'planted' in the desert."

In 1949 Lincoln Fitzgerald, then owner of the Nevada Club in Reno and said to have been an accountant for Detroit's Purple Gang, survived being gunned down by shotgun blasts in Reno as he opened his garage door. He later bought the Tahoe Biltmore in Crystal Bay and also built Fitzgerald's in Reno. An unsubstantiated story tells of a second assassination attempt on Fitzgerald at Tahoe Meadows while he rode in a car with two bodyguards.

The Senate Committee on Organized Crime, commonly referred to as the Kefauver Commission, after holding meetings in cities across the country, came to Las Vegas for meetings in 1950. Many of the figures "of interest" had suddenly been called out of town and were not available for questioning; others remembered or knew nothing to which they could attest. Although less effective than had been hoped, the meetings led officials to conclude that America's two major crime syndicates were operating in Nevada. In doing so, they may have inadvertently helped the industry: confirming public suspicion and enhancing the attraction for some casinogoers who wished to rub shoulders with, or at least catch a glimpse of, "Joe Batters," "Momo," or "Trigger Mike."

Fearful of the specter of federal regulation, in 1955 the state initiated its first halting efforts to manage the gambling industry by creating the State Gaming Control Board, and in 1960 Governor Grant Sawyer introduced the "black book," which banned notorious organized-crime figures.

The most spectacular casino-related murder occurred in August 1968.

Richard Chartrand, who was the managing owner of Barney's Club and also had an interest in the Tahoe Nugget, got in his Cadillac in the Nevada Skyland development, on Tahoe's southeast shore. As he pulled out of the driveway, the drag of a one-pound fishing weight tightened a line that pulled a guitar pick from between electrical terminals. When the terminals touched, they detonated a battery-powered bomb under the car's floorboard. It was rumored that Chartrand had been skimming money from Barney's.

The FBI and the Los Angeles police assisted local police in investigating the crime. Authorities came to believe two career criminals from Southern California were the perpetrators. The criminals had traveled to the area shortly before the assassination and returned to Los Angeles the day after. They possessed knowledge of dynamite, had records of violence, and apparently acted at the behest of one of the victim's hidden partners. Lacking any physical evidence, the district attorney could not prosecute. One person of interest declined to discuss the matter, explaining, "I don't want a bullet or two in my head." Nevada has been much more effective in policing the gambling industry since 1970, and since then reports of connections between the underworld and the Tahoe casinos have not been publicly circulated.

Wealthy sportsmen had been racing hydroplanes on the lake since the 1920s when the *Lucky Strike II* shattered West Coast records, running more than 80 miles per hour. The rules were "play for keeps" in the early

The *Miss Seattle* racing in 1957. The hydro hulls sped over the lake at more than 100 miles per hour. (Courtesy Special Collections, University of Nevada, Reno, Library)

days. Stories proliferated of steel grindings in carburetor intakes and sea cocks inexplicably opening so that race boats sank to the bottom of their boathouse wells. By the 1950s, with security undoubtedly tighter, ten thousand to fifteen thousand spectators lined the west shore to watch *Skipalong of California* and *Short Snorter* duel *Hawaii Kai* and *Breathless*. The hydro hulls allowed speeds of well over 100 miles per hour, and in August 1953 the *Hurricane IV* screamed down Tahoe's Mile High Race straightaway at 140 miles per hour.

Racing continued at the lake into the mid-1960s. For several years Harrah's Club sponsored the only bistate unlimited hydroplane race in the country, and Bill Harrah's *Tahoe Miss* always contended.

While summer speedboat racing was limited to the well-to-do, and later to those with large corporate sponsors, winter sports were expanding so they might better include the general population. In 1947, at Tahoe City, a Norwegian ski jumper and former sea captain named Kjell "Rusty" Rustad built Granlibakken nearly single-handedly. With a handful of friends he cleared the hill, built a log cabin and a bridge to get across a stream, installed a 450-foot rope to the top, and began hosting the Lake Tahoe Ski Club as well as young locals who would grow up on skis. Meanwhile, Wayne Poulsen had created the Squaw Valley Ski Resort, which opened on Thanksgiving Day 1949. Its main attraction came to be the mountain face dubbed "KT 22." Poulsen named it after watching his wife, Sandy, an experienced skier, descend utilizing twenty-two kick turns (the KT in the name), one after each traverse of the breathtakingly steep run.

In 1948 Poulsen had recruited an investor from the East, Alex Cushing, to form the Squaw Valley Development Corporation. Shortly before the mountain opened for business, a bitter dispute broke up the partnership. Cushing, who owned 52 percent of the stock, called a stockholders meeting while Poulsen, the president, was out of town and ousted him. Cushing, the company's secretary-treasurer, took over control, and Poulsen never made a cent directly from the resort that had been his dream. Fortunately for Poulsen, he owned a majority of the land on the valley floor, and he did very well in the real estate business. His son said he often heard his father comment, "It doesn't matter; besides the fish are rising and the skiing is fine. Come on, boys, it's time to go!"

At its opening Squaw Valley comprised a small lodge, one rope tow, and the longest double chairlift in the world. During the first five years of operation, three avalanches ripped out lift towers, there were four bridge washouts, and twice the lodge flooded. Still, in 1954, when Cushing learned that Reno had bid for the 1960 Olympic Games, he thought it would be a great publicity stunt to submit his own bid. He found he needed to make a formal presentation to the Olympic Committee the following month. Working fast, he gained the California governor's assistance and persuaded the state legislature to revive an old bill that promised money for the Los Angeles 1932 Summer Olympics. The legislature amended the outdated bill, guaranteeing one million dollars for the Winter Games. Cushing made his proposal, selling the idea of the uniqueness of a virgin mountain with an annual snowfall of 450 inches.

Although one Olympic Committee member called it "a glorified picnic ground," Squaw Valley became the U.S. nominee over Lake Placid, Sun Valley, and Aspen. Avery Brundage, the president of the International Olympic Committee, commented that the U.S. committee "obviously has taken leave of their senses." When he heard how minimal the facilities at Squaw Valley were, he muttered, "This is worse than I thought. If you win the Games, you'll set the Olympics back 25 years."

The Squaw Valley contingent now faced the impossible task of convincing the International Olympic Committee that it would be able to host an Olympics. The area had nothing to compare with the facilities in Europe, where the Games were traditionally held. Even one of the U.S. representatives let it be known they would not vote for their own nominee. The other contenders included the Bavaria resort that had hosted the 1936 Olympics; St. Moritz, Switzerland; and the favorite, Innsbruck, Austria. The Tahoe resort had to rely on its impressive mountain and the bluster of its advocate.

Cushing hired associates to lobby European and Scandinavian representatives as well as those of South America, who ordinarily cared little about the Winter Games. In Europe Jo Marillac, a mountain climber and skier who had been named France's greatest all-around athlete in 1950, effectively touted the U.S. case. The members of the International Federation of Skiing greatly respected Marillac, a war hero who had fought with the French Resistance. He had begun working at Squaw Valley in

1953, and his enthusiasm for its runs and deep powder convinced the federation to support the fledgling resort's effort. Cushing won over Brundage, who in turn won over some international delegates.

The decisive meeting took place in Paris in June 1955. Confident, Innsbruck had begun notifying various delegations of their housing accommodations. The U.S. bid, written in French, English, and Spanish, promoted the idea that the Olympics needed to be a worldwide event, not merely the domain of one continent. After the other two nominees were eliminated on the first ballot, Innsbruck and the upstart Squaw Valley remained as the choices. On the second ballot, to shock and disbelief, the Tahoe site won the bid, thirty-two votes to ten. The resort now had four and a half years to design and build roads, bridges, housing, restaurants, ski lifts, ski jumps, cross-country courses, a speed-skating track, and an ice arena.

As Squaw Valley undertook this daunting task, the expansion of another Tahoe ski area made news on the lake's south shore. Chris Kuraisa, owner of a local sporting-goods store, leased land from the Forest Service and built a chairlift above the Bijou Ski Run, a rope-tow hill. He named the area Heavenly Valley. Taking an active part in cutting trees, pouring cement, and erecting the lift's twenty-six towers, Kuraisa and his construction team completed the sixteen-hundred-foot vertical lift in the summer of 1955. His hill opened for business with the December snows. Because looking down the steep fall line of the mountain face was like sighting down the barrel of a gun, Kuraisa named the soon-to-be-renowned run "Gunbarrel." The first year Heavenly Valley netted $23,000, charging $4 for an all-day pass to ride the chairlift.

Besides leasing land to ski resorts, the Forest Service looked to develop public uses of other federal lands in the basin. In the mid-1950s it had an opportunity to purchase 750 acres of marsh habitat at the mouth of the lake's largest tributary, the Upper Truckee River. The asking price was $75,000. Conservation had not yet become a priority, and, seeing no value in obtaining the swampy south-shore meadow, the Forest Service rejected the proposal. In December 1956 the Lincoln Development Company bought the property to create Tahoe Keys, billed as a "fabulous beach-front development." The plan included excavating 150-foot-wide "lagoons" in the meadow so the two thousand homesites, on fingers of

Until the 1960s the Upper Truckee River marsh acted as a natural filter, keeping sediment from entering the lake. (Courtesy Special Collections, University of Nevada, Reno, Library)

land, would have water access to the lake. This allowed all homes in the upscale tract to be advertised as "waterfront."

A year and a half later, new houses opened on a road leading to the meadow, with dredging of the canals following shortly thereafter. The Upper Truckee River was reengineered to run directly into the lake. A newspaper article five years later reported that research by the Dillingham Corporation, which now owned the project, had still not found a chemical or mechanical treatment that could prevent "turbid material," including sediments and nutrients, from flowing into the lake. The loss of the marshland as a natural filter proved to be the single largest disruption to the lake's watershed since the clear-cutting of its forests.

A few miles east, in Nevada, planners sought to ease a traffic bottleneck. America's love affair with the automobile had intensified, and federal funds were available to modernize highways. At the same time, Nevada wanted an area for summer boating access and picnicking on the south shore. Planners determined that by blasting a second tunnel through Cave Rock, a portion of the displaced granite could be used for a roadway to the lake's edge as well as a boat ramp. The cost of the dual projects would be $455,717, split between the State of Nevada and the federal government.

As in the earlier tunnel building, Washoe Indians had no access to the land-use agencies, and no one consulted them in the decision. On October 11, 1956, bidding began for the second excavation. The first tunnel was 153 feet long; the new one, closer to the main cave's face, would be 410 feet. The federal Bureau of Public Roads had financed the removal of thousands of cubic yards of earth on the approaches to the new bore. This material had been used to begin building the access road to the lake. The newspaper in nearby Gardnerville touted the roadside project, saying, "The park is expected to be one of Douglas County's prime attractions for tourists, meeting a long-recognized need for additional free public recreational facilities on the lakeshore."

By December workers were attacking the rock from the north and south. The use of explosives had gained precision since 1931. Each shot, using 450 pounds of dynamite, blasted eight feet from the rock. After each detonation, fired alternately in the north and south bores, workers removed the debris and set timbering for the next.

Washoe Indians saw the new project as adding insult to injury. Fifty years later Washoe elder Ruth Abbie spoke of the tribe's reaction to the tunnel. Believing that the "Great Spirit" had given Lake Tahoe to the Washoes, the tribe tried to hang on to it, she said, but the government did what it wanted, calling it progress. She described Cave Rock as "that naturally pristine site," and said, "They never inquired of the Washoes. Do you understand how strongly the Washoes feel about that? When we try to fight for the little we have left, the sacred spots, well, it's just like talking in the wind."

The Washoes believe only shamans should access Cave Rock and that its misuse puts people in jeopardy. That winter's project did not dispel the notion, as accidents plagued the project. A bulldozer rolled down a steep embankment on a nearby grade. A foreman, on the mountain side of the highway, slammed the door of his truck, and the emergency brake released. The truck rolled across the road, catapulted over the nearly perpendicular embankment, tumbled, and plunged into the lake. And, sometime later, without warning, a five-hundred-pound rock careened down the monolith's granite face, crushing a worker's leg.

Its proved difficult to keep superintendents on the project; three were employed at different times. The original proposal called for completion of the job by June 1, well in advance of the heavy summer travel. With the ongoing problems, officials repeatedly postponed the opening: to June 15, July 15, August 5, and finally August 16, when they announced its completion.

A few miles south, the evolving gaming industry was driving the lake's growth. In 1955–56 revenues for Douglas County, primarily from the lake's Harrah's Club and Harvey's Wagon Wheel, totaled more than seven million dollars. Harrah's buses began transporting patrons for free from Stockton and Sacramento, three times daily, seven days a week. The need of support services for its expanding tourism ensured a population boom for the area. In 1953 the Tahoe Paradise Corporation purchased sixteen hundred acres of land, encompassing Meyers at the base of Johnson Pass, and opened its first subdivision in 1955. By 1957, on the south shore alone, there were forty real estate agents and an estimated one thousand new motel and hotel units being added yearly. New subdivisions offered lots for fifteen dollars down and fifteen dollars a month.

Noting the growth, some wondered about regulating the basin's development. In January 1957 the *Sacramento Bee* ran a five-part series titled "The Tahoe Problem." The articles posed this question: "How can the beauty and recreation value of the area be protected in the face of demands for logging and expanded building?"

In September of that year the *Bee* reported that the problem was being considered in at least one quarter: San Francisco lawyer William D. Evers had formed the nonprofit Tahoe Improvement and Conservation Association. Evers, the president of the one-hundred-member organization, said the group wanted to preserve the area and keep it beautiful. Their concerns included everything from planning and zoning to water quality. Although not opposed to growth, Evers stressed that without controls, it would destroy the value of the area. His group, the forerunner to the "Keep Tahoe Blue" organization, the League to Save Lake Tahoe, had started a decades-long crusade to influence the forces of development, engaging in battles that continue to the present day.

Chapter Nine

The 1960s

$\mathcal{B}$y 1960 Tahoe boosters had much to crow about. The resident population had surged from 2,850 in 1956 to 12,000. Building was advancing in all five basin counties; El Dorado County alone approved five thousand new subdivided lots in Tahoe. The Crystal Bay Development Company had purchased nine thousand acres from which they were creating Incline Village. Besides its residences, schools, and shopping centers, the Incline community plan incorporated the Luggi Foeger–designed ski area, beaches, and a Robert Trent Jones–designed golf course.

Improvements to tourist resorts included Harrah's Club's $3.5 million South Shore Room. The spacious theater-restaurant, with its large stage and "flyway" area, allowed the production of any kind of show, and its headliners included the best entertainers in show business, from comedian Jimmy Durante and performer Liberace to singer Patti Page—the opening act of the new year. At the same time, Harvey's Resort and Casino expanded operations to include an eleven-story hotel. It now boasted more slot machines under one roof than any other place in the world. Even with the area's spectacular growth, as the year began chamber of commerce officials were troubled. The lake's worldwide showcase opportunity, the Olympic Games, was scheduled for mid-February, and the winter had produced little snow by New Year's Day.

Finally, on January 7, the *Tahoe Daily Tribune* announced an approaching storm that, the paper predicted, would bring heavy snow. Within a few days there were eighteen inches of snow on the valley floor with more coming. Over the next three weeks storm followed heavy storm, until at the end of the month Squaw Valley had a twenty-foot snowpack. The newspaper now reported that the Olympic Committee, "anxious earlier that there would be no snow," now worried that the area was becoming "snow-clogged." Operations at Squaw Valley were hampered by the continuous storms, which seemed a good problem.

Suddenly, on February 7, days before the Olympic opening, a warmer storm battered the Sierra. Winds up to one hundred miles per hour preceded torrential rains. Five and a half inches of rain fell in South Lake Tahoe, causing $500,000 in damages. Trees were uprooted and power poles snapped. At the Olympic site six inches of rain washed away the lower portion of the downhill course, and flooding carried off several small buildings. Trailers and a three-hundred-pound decorative statue were toppled. Squaw Creek cut through the main parking lot, buckling its surface, leading to speculation that it could not be repaired before the spectators arrived. For the first time ever, all athletes were housed under one roof, Olympic Village Inn; with the deluge, they sat confined in their rooms.

Officials were frantic. Then, the following afternoon, nature again reversed course, and the rain turned into snow. Within twenty-four hours ten to fifteen inches again covered the valley floor. At the Olympic site, workers struggled frantically to mend the damages as skiing, jumping, and skating practices were postponed or canceled. The U.S. military was called in to repair the parking lots.

Snow continued off and on for the next ten days, but the workers completed their tasks, and the athletes managed to test the courses. Although there was an abundance of fresh powder, things looked bleak for the opening of the Games on February 18, as the area was plagued with heavy flurries. At eight o'clock that morning traffic was jammed. With chains required, cars inched along. Slowly, the parking lots filled, and just as the Games were declared open, the storm broke and the sky cleared. Walt Disney, head of pageantry, orchestrated the release of two thousand doves. As four thousand California and Nevada high school band and choral members played and sang, the Olympic flame was lit.

Notable in the ceremonies was the fact that figure skater Carol Heiss, who would win the gold medal, became the first female to take the Olympic oath on behalf of all the athletes.

The Games were a great success. They were the first to include women's speed skating and a biathlon event, which combined cross-country skiing and rifle marksmanship. With all the athletes living under the same roof, camaraderie was established across national bounds. Seeing Italians, Americans, and Russians together called to mind the sportsmanship that the Olympics are intended to foster. Despite snow snarling traffic over the course of the Games, an estimated 240,000 people attended. A record 47,000 spectators filled the valley on one day.

In a cold war drama the U.S. hockey team defeated the defending-champion Russians three to two in a thrilling, come-from-behind semi-final match. Although disputed by some team members, an often-repeated story tells of the Russian captain coming into the American locker room before the last period of the final game, with the United States losing to Czechoslovakia four to three. The Russian reportedly signaled with hand gestures that the players should inhale from the oxygen tank he carried. Most did, rejuvenating themselves. Whether that account is accurate or not, the "Team of Destiny" came out and scored six goals to win their first hockey gold medal, nine to four.

Four years after being called a "glorified picnic ground," Squaw Valley prepared to host the Olympic Games. (Courtesy Special Collections, University of Nevada, Reno, Library)

The Games were televised daily nationwide for the first time ever, exposing millions of viewers to the area's beauty, establishing it as a world-class destination. The Reno airport, today's Reno/Tahoe International Airport, in operation since 1929, built its first terminal for the Games, and rooms throughout the Greater Reno–Carson City area were full for the entire ten-day event. A veteran observer commented, "It beats everything we ever saw, even in the middle of the summer tourist season." The south shore did not do quite as well filling its rooms but used the Games as a marketing coup. A Harrah's Club publicist said, "We considered the Olympics a great opportunity to get Lake Tahoe's name out to the world and to get Harrah's name out at the same time. It did the job. Everybody knew where it was, and from then on business was great."

While the Games established Tahoe's reputation as a scenic wonder, Squaw Valley's ultimate success became problematic and would remain so for a long time. California had spent millions, including the state's $1 million contingency fund, to construct the Games' facilities. When would the huge investment be repaid? One assemblywoman had called the project a "white elephant." An assemblyman said, "I'm sick of this Squaw Valley deal and I think every other legislator is." Wayne Poulsen believed the problem lay with his former partner, saying the valley was "at the whim and mercy of one man." That man, Alex Cushing, said, "Dealing with state and federal politics was a terrible situation. It was chaos." It would take ten years to sort out the disorder.

At the basin's other major ski resort, Heavenly Valley, things ran much smoother. In the spring of 1960 Chris Kuraisa built a lift to the top of Monument Peak, adding six thousand feet to his resort. The addition, which cost $300,000, would provide up to two extra months of skiing, one in early winter and another in the spring. Kuraisa hired the world-renowned Stein Ericson to promote the resort. At the same time, he set up school programs and provided free passes to underprivileged children so "every kid could ski." Two years later he built the largest aerial tramway in America. It ran all year, affording spectacular views of the lake to sightseers as well as greater access to the mountain for skiers.

Other projects were the subject of interest in the spring of 1960. In April, at Tahoe Keys, contracts were let for underground power lines and water mains. The project was running ahead of schedule. Earthmoving had been done seven days a week throughout the winter. Dredging and fill operations were complete for six of the proposed twenty-nine keys, so that 296 homesites were created on the lagoons.

Another major construction project brought state senators to Tahoe for discussions. The proposal of a $4 million highway around the west shore included building a bridge across the mouth of Emerald Bay. The limitations of the roadway around the lake were apparent to all on the first day of the Olympic Games. With snow falling, road conditions through the morning could be summarized as "closed, open, closed." When it opened, cars were forced to inch along the narrow road that had been built thirty years earlier. Now, newspapers reported that 100 percent of the local population supported the proposed project.

The South Shore Chamber of Commerce issued a proclamation that included the viewpoint that the bridge would not "detract one iota from the beauty of Emerald Bay." In fact, the organization argued, the bridge would furnish the visitor a more spectacular view than the current road. The project would involve adding fill along the edge of the lake and perhaps creating an eleven-hundred-foot electrically lit tunnel. A week later

In the 1960s the Upper Truckee River marsh was dredged to create lagoons and two thousand beachfront home-sites. The loss of the marsh added dramatically to the deterioration of Lake Tahoe's clarity. (Courtesy Special Collections, University of Nevada, Reno, Library)

the *Tahoe Daily Tribune* front-page headline stated, "Emerald Bay Bridge Prospects Look Favorable." The opposition to the proposal, according to the paper, came from elsewhere, "notably the state division of beaches and parks." The perception that locals were in conflict with "out-of-towners" and that local governments and businesses would have to fight against state and federal agencies escalated through the years.

On the north shore one business garnered colorful publicity that soon turned to notoriety. In September 1960 a group bought the Cal Neva. The partnership included Frank Sinatra and his associates: Paul "Skinny" D'Amato, owner of Atlantic City's infamous 500 Club; Miami's Sanford Waterman, later convicted of racketeering; and an alleged silent partner, underworld figure Sam Giancana. The new owners invested a reported $3.5 million in renovations. Of particular note were the Celebrity Show-room, with its helicopter pad on the roof, and underground tunnels to guest bungalows. Sinatra's influence brought entertainment stars to the casino that rivaled Harrah's across the lake. Friends Dean Martin, Joey Bishop, and Eddie Fisher headlined, as did elite performers like Lena Horne and Ella Fitzgerald. Sinatra's tenure as owner of the Cal Neva is replete with stories involving Mafioso pit bosses, skimming, prostitution, orgies, brawls, and FBI surveillance.

Marilyn Monroe spent a week at the lodge just prior to her tragic death in Los Angeles. Differing accounts of who she was with during that week continue to provoke interest. Sinatra engaged in at least two fistfights at the resort, including one with a former deputy sheriff who died in a mysterious car crash shortly thereafter.

The July 1963 Cal Neva appearance of the McGuire Sisters doomed Sinatra's ownership of the resort. Giancana, prominent in Nevada's "black book" listing of those banned from its casinos, visited girlfriend Phyllis McGuire and stayed in one of the resort's bungalows. The breach initiated an investigation by the Nevada Gaming Control Board that prompted an attempted bribe of its agents by Sinatra's associate D'Amato and threats by Sinatra. The threats were issued against Edward A. Olsen, Gaming Board chairman, and were delivered using language described as "vile, indecent, foul, repulsive, and venomous in the extreme." Olsen later commented, "I had never heard some of the things he called me."

Sinatra's injudicious attempt at intimidation added to the list of Cal

The Cal Neva Resort, Spa, and Casino, shown here in the 1950s, is located in Crystal Bay, Lake Tahoe. It is the only property in Lake Tahoe located on the state lines of California and Nevada. (Courtesy Special Collections, University of Nevada, Reno, Library)

Neva violations. The affair resulted in the entertainer's forfeiting his state gaming license and closing the resort on Labor Day 1963. It reopened in 1964, under new ownership, but a number of local businesses closed with Sinatra's departure.

In spite of the problems at any specific resort, in the first years of the 1960s, Tahoe's resident population jumped another 25 percent. At the north end of the lake from July 1, 1961, to April 1, 1962, building permits were issued for $14.8 million, including one for $5 million worth of streets, water, and sewage for Incline Village. In 1963 there were sixteen thousand full-time inhabitants in the basin. Projections estimated the population would continue to grow even more rapidly and that by 1970 there would be thirty-six thousand residents.

Calls for action to protect the lake's ecology came from other parts of California. The *Sacramento Bee* commented, "The virus of urban sprawl is encroaching upon the green forests around the lake." In several articles it echoed sentiments from its 1957 series on the issues facing the Lake Tahoe area. It pointed out that the lake's natural beauty; the Division of Highways' decision to keep Highway 50 over Echo Summit open during the winter, providing easy access; real estate speculation, which had become a major industry; the rapid expansion of gambling casinos; and aggressive promotional campaigns combined to make it "the fastest growing area in the nation." The paper called the effects on what had been a remote, peaceful alpine area "devastating." An article in the *Los Angeles Times* came under the headline "Action to Save Tahoe Is Urgent."

It had become apparent to those studying its growth that governing the unique region was impossible. Lake Tahoe fell under the jurisdiction of two states, five counties, many special districts, and sixty local agencies. The groups were fragmented, their decisions often merely dilatory, and consensus among them unachievable.

In 1958 the Lake Tahoe Area Council was formed. It was a nonprofit organization, established with the sponsorship of Nevada's Max C. Fleischmann Foundation. Dedicated to the preservation and orderly development of the Lake Tahoe Basin, the council was instrumental in basinwide air- and water-pollution studies. In 1963, after extensive work, the council issued a preliminary regional plan. It made suggestions for orderly urban expansion, pointing out that "preservation of the scenic beauty of the Basin is essential to the economic growth and development of the area." Although the various governmental commissions and boards may have agreed with the sentiment, they did not accept specific policy proposals, and the plan was never implemented.

In June 1965 four dirt breakwaters were built at Crystal Bay on the north shore, without Nevada's approval. No one knew if the state had legal recourse to stop the builders. In previous similar cases, small fines had been assessed, causing one official to complain of the encroachment on public domain, "The punishment in these cases does not fit the crime. For once a fill is in, it cannot be removed or the damage repaired. It becomes a permanent liability to the lake."

At the same time, on the south shore, an editorial in the *Tahoe Daily Tribune* titled "Time to Think Big!" argued that the area's ski facilities topped those of the state of Colorado. Although Americans believed Colorado was the biggest and best state for skiing, the editorial stated, by the following winter Tahoe would have thirty-four chairlifts or trams, while the entire state of Colorado had only thirty-one. Tahoe needed to advertise across the country, not only for its gaming—which over the previous ten years had carried the burden of promotion—but also for its giant recreation industry. The paper touted a "bold $100,000 national advertising" campaign to increase the number of visitors to the lake.

In November 1965 the Reno City Council passed a resolution opposing "any increase in population density, exportation of water or sewage, and increased pollution" at Tahoe. Specifically, the council objected to a north-shore developer's request to increase the area's allowable population density for a real estate development. Approval would increase water use and sewage. Because the Truckee River, flowing out of Tahoe, was Reno's primary water source, anything affecting the lake affected Reno.

Another large expansion at the south shore had begun in 1964: the Del Webb Corporation's fourteen-story, $25 million Sahara Tahoe Casino. Webb, one of America's most successful builders and financiers, had appeared on the cover of *Time* when creating his Sun City retirement communities. His career also included winning government contracts from the Department of Defense and building one of the early Las Vegas hotels, the Flamingo. An apparent Mob hit killed Bugsy Siegel, one of the Flamingo's owners, just weeks after its grand opening. Webb claimed he did not know about Siegel's association with the Mob, although he noted that Siegel had paid for the work in cash.

The Sahara Tahoe was one of five casinos Webb owned in Nevada, which made him the largest employer in the state. Publicized as the lake's first Vegas-style casino, the Sahara opened with gala New Year's Eve–type festivities at midnight on July 1, 1965. It began immediately competing with Harrah's for top entertainment, soon landing Elvis Presley as one of its multi-night headliners.

Shortly after the completion of the Sahara Tahoe, an intense and acrimonious campaign led to the incorporation of the south shore. The California side of Stateline, Bijou, Al Tahoe, and Tahoe Valley joined to form the City of South Lake Tahoe.

Those favoring cityhood raised the issue of the area's lack of representation in county government and planning. Only one of five El Dorado County supervisors came from the Tahoe Basin, as did only one of eight county planners. All others represented areas on the western slope of the Sierra. This was despite the fact that the Tahoe portion had one-third of the county's population and more than half its assessed valuation. A group called the Lake Valley Taxpayers Association was vocal in opposing incorporation.

Stateline at night in the 1960s. (Courtesy Special Collections, University of Nevada, Reno, Library)

The taxpayer association argued that the county governed effectively and did it cheaper than a city would. Only a portion of Lake Valley, including an estimated 11,000 to 15,000 people, had been included in the incorporation plan, because large property owners outside the heavily populated south shore were against the proposal. The taxpayer association argued that the area lacked size for a city, and it would have no ability to control growth outside its boundaries. As the election approached and the popularity of passing the issue became more apparent, the association introduced scare tactics, accusing the incorporators of having ulterior motives. "Could this be a real-estate land grab?" asked one in a series of newspaper advertisements. Another asked, "How much will your taxes go up each year?" The public was not getting the unbiased truth, and costs had been grossly underestimated, the association charged. "There is no absolute limit to city taxes," it warned.

Arguments for incorporation featured home rule, emphasizing 100 percent representation rather than 20 percent, the need to get more services for taxes collected, and better planning and control to save the area's natural beauty. "Stop the hodge-podge development and exploitation, and instead have more orderly growth," read an ad in favor of incorporation. To counter the charge that special interests were pushing the proposal, proincorporation ads included this disclaimer: "Paid for by scores of small donors." The vote was a landslide favoring the formation of the city, 2,011 to 614. Touting itself as the highest California city, South Lake Tahoe became an official incorporated area on November 30, 1965. The taxpayer association's fears proved to be unfounded, but so did the promise of orderly growth.

Developing the roadway around the lake's west shore remained a hot topic. In 1966 the California Division of Highways proposed a four-lane freeway, and the state highway engineer continued lobbying for a bridge across Emerald Bay. The State Park Commission denounced the proposals, and newspapers throughout Northern California objected to them. The director of the Lake Tahoe Area Council argued that preservation of the lake should not be subordinated to improving transit. The arguments continued for several years, and each year, as state funds were allocated to other California traffic projects, the west shore and Emerald Bay work was deferred. Eventually, the state reduced the undertaking to the reinforcement of the two-lane road in slide areas.

In 1968 conservationists succeeded in getting Emerald Bay designated a National Natural Landmark. During the dustup, an El Dorado County supervisor from Tahoe suggested it was not conservationists but the government that was trying to "slip one by." The battle between local and regional interests was intensifying.

Chapter Ten

At Cross-Purposes

*F*rom the late 1960s through the '70s and '80s, Lake Tahoe presented a cheerful aspect to the world. The Ponderosa Ranch theme park, at Incline Village, which started out as the stable for horses for the *Bonanza* television show, hosted thousands of visitors each year. Over the course of ten years, millions of viewers watched John Denver's Celebrity Ski Classic at Heavenly Valley as big-name celebrities hammed it up on the slopes and, paired with professional racers, skied against one another. Top entertainers performed at the casinos, and, depending on the season, the slopes or the beaches were filled. While chambers of commerce touted the lake as the ultimate destination resort, behind-the-scenes battles raged.

Tahoe had become a classic case of entities working at cross-purposes. People outside the basin, as well as conservationists inside its bounds, were attempting to protect the lake, and area businesspeople continued to work to build it up and promote it.

In California, in 1967, Democratic state assemblyman Edwin L. Z'berg, honored later by having his name added to Sugar Pine Point State Park on the west shore, introduced a bill to create the California Tahoe Regional Planning Agency (CTRPA). Its role would be to set pollution standards and regulate land use. W. Brad Murphy, the first mayor of the city of South Lake Tahoe, had pledged to block further "hodgepodge" urbanization, but local officials and taxpayers' associations strongly

objected to Z'berg's plan. They called a regional government unrealistic and deemed it unnecessary.

In a meeting of the California General Assembly, one of the city's former mayors insisted the problems could be solved locally. Speaking of the lake, he remarked, "It is still blue." A representative of a taxpayers' group commented that the proposal of a regional agency was "tyrannical." He said, "It would throw government back to the dark ages." A Democratic assemblyman countered wryly, "Lake Tahoe was a lot more attractive in those days."

Lobbied to support the formation of the CTRPA by the League to Save Lake Tahoe (the League) and the League of Women Voters, among others, the legislature approved the agency. In practice, the CTRPA's achievements were limited for two reasons: It governed only the lake's California side, and its composition was designed to keep control in local hands. Of its five members, two represented the local counties and a third the City of South Lake Tahoe. Those three entities generally wanted continued development, and most frequently voted as a bloc.

This threw meaningful regulation, if it were to be achieved, to the federal government. The U.S. Congress acted by creating the Tahoe Regional Planning Agency (TRPA), a bistate organization, which convened in March 1970. It had been a yearlong struggle to create the agency, and in the meantime building and expansion had continued apace. The Nevada author of the agreement that formed the TRPA, state senator Coe Swobe, said Tahoe had undergone "an out-of-control boom." At its approval Californian Z'berg commented, "[The federal plan] gives us a chance of saving this great, incomparable resource." A *Modesto Bee* editorial commented, "The hour is late."

The TRPA's powers over local governments were unequaled anywhere in the country. As years passed it issued regulations, disregarded them, and revised them. The agency failed but was subsequently reconstituted, enduring tribulations, attacks, and lawsuits foisted on it from both sides of the political spectrum.

Four months after its formation, developers, who challenged the agency's attempt to limit growth, brought the first lawsuit against the TRPA. Private properties on steep slopes and in stream zones, whose development would cause silt to wash into the lake, promoting algae growth, were downzoned. This infuriated owners and businesspeople, who viewed the regulations as an unjustified intrusion on private property rights. When properties were classified unbuildable, owners labeled the condemnations unconstitutional and un-American. The officials on the TRPA board were sensitive to this argument and decided to allow building on certain high-hazard lands if contractors ensured proper drainage and utilized native materials. Those who wanted building controlled now filed suits claiming that no real restrictions were being enforced.

Notwithstanding the chorus of disapproval, in the 1970s in nearly all respects, the TRPA was a toothless entity. During its first fifteen months of existence, it approved 99 percent of building applications. Like the CTRPA, local representatives dominated it, and its rules were designed to sanction growth. A majority of both states' representatives was necessary to prevent a project from moving forward. This meant if 30 percent of the board voted for a project, as long as it was three of the five from one state, approval was granted. Further, if the agency did not reach agreement within sixty days, the venture automatically gained approval.

In May 1971 environmentalists denounced the TRPA's authorization of three projects: a 250-unit Incline Village development to be built on slopes of 40 percent to 50 percent, a 942-unit townhouse development at Carnelian Bay, and Harrah's Club's eighteen-story high-rise hotel, intended to be the tallest building at the lake. When asked about the Harrah's project, a board member, also a South Lake Tahoe city councilman, explained, "It's not our prerogative to dictate to them as long as they say they're going to do the best job possible. We're dealing with an organization which is highly reputable."

At the same time, studies of the lake by limnologist Charles Goldman were beginning to be more widely recognized and accepted. His findings would eventually be used in state, national, and international policy decisions around the globe, earning him prestigious awards, including the Albert Einstein World Award of Science. At the presentation of this award, it was noted that Goldman's environmental research program at Lake Tahoe brought "true benefit to mankind." In 1974 Goldman reported the shocking finding that since 1960 the lake had lost 25 percent of its clarity.

In August 1974 the lake's casinos entertained 63,000 people a day. Their patronage that year totaled 13,792,000. Still, the TRPA approved four new hotel-casino projects at Stateline on the south shore. The League sued to prevent their construction, citing the fact that increased traffic would exceed federal air-pollution standards. Although an air study showed that carbon monoxide from summer holiday traffic topped that of Los Angeles at the height of smog season, since the projects had been approved by the ruling agency, the court rejected the suit.

Between 1960 and 1974, without comprehensive regulations, the lake lost 25 percent of its clarity. In the middle of South Tahoe, this drainage pipe from Highway 50 into the lake still existed in 1992. (Courtesy Laurel Ames)

Between 1970 and 1978 dwelling units increased from 20,263 to 36,043. Incoming traffic increased 80 percent. Concentrations of air pollutants exceeded federal levels thirty-three times in 1976 and seventy times in 1977. The most powerful lawmaker in the California legislature, Leo McCarthy, visited the lake in the spring of 1976. He charged that the TRPA was fronting for construction and gambling interests and threatened to pursue stronger federal legislation.

In the meantime, the TRPA had been revised so that a majority of its members were appointed regional board members rather than local officials. When the state passed the California Environmental Quality Act of 1970, projects were required to submit documentation of their potential environmental impacts. With the amending of the state's Clean Air Act in 1977, Tahoe was designated a nonattainment area—its concentration of air pollutants doubling from the previous year—and regulations were tightened further. Typical local officials' reactions to the CTRPA were displayed at a South Tahoe City Council meeting when one member attacked the agency for implying that local government was not looking out for its citizens' best interests and another accused the agency of being "a tin god."

By June 1977, of the four new casino projects approved earlier, three were ready to move forward. Two of the three construction sites at the south shore's Stateline had been cleared. In addition, Harvey's had gained approval for a twenty-two-story 550-room expansion that included a parking garage. The *Sacramento Bee* titled an editorial "More Casinos at Tahoe Are Absolute Madness." The editor argued that the addition of the approved Nevada construction, with support services, would double the south shore's population. The piece concluded, "If Tahoe is destroyed for the sake of building more gambling casinos, future generations will look back to this generation with anger and dismay."

Lawsuits again stopped the building temporarily. Lake Tahoe Forest Service supervisor Bill Morgan held a press conference proposing that one way to resolve the problem would be for someone to buy the casino sites. In the end, Nevada and the federal government each contributed more than ten million dollars, and two of the three new sites were purchased and retired. At the same time developers, real estate agents, businesspeople, and a large group of property owners were seeking ways to pursue other projects; in California that meant curbing or circumventing the CTRPA's regulations. "There isn't an environmental problem at the lake," said one of the prodevelopment leaders, Terry Trupp. "What the lake suffers from is political pollution."

Trupp, the executive director of a group that called itself the Council for Logic, said he received calls every day from people who had retired and invested in Tahoe in good faith, only to be denied use of their property. Trupp started a campaign urging individuals to withhold paying their taxes. "The [TRPA] is non-elected and has jurisdiction over local residents. It means the rights of the State are supreme," he said. And he concluded, "Folks' dreams are going up in smoke."

One man, determined to keep his dream from evaporating, took matters into his own hands. Bob Pershing had moved to the lake a few years earlier from Los Angeles, where he worked as a mason. He owned a one-acre lot in a CTRPA-designated stream zone on the Upper Truckee River. Pershing called the CTRPA a "Gestapo-type" agency and refused to apply for building permits. Supported by the Council for Logic and several businesses that donated materials, he began constructing a five-bedroom house, using pickup loads of dirt fill to landscape a yard in what had been wetland along the river. Pershing said, "No one has a right to dictate to a man what he can put on his property." Trupp remarked, "Bob has become a symbol—a symbol of guts."

On successive weekends contractors from throughout the south shore arrived at Pershing's construction site, pounding nails and lifting walls, in violation of the agencies' regulations. The assistance was successful as a demonstration of support, but it weakened a time later, as Pershing went to jail for defying building codes. The forty-two-hundred-square-foot house was enclosed but would remain unfinished inside for twenty years. Pershing's wife later commented, "At that time we thought if the contractors would get behind him maybe we could run the [regional regulators] out of town. But Bob was the only one. Only he went to jail, he went alone."

Another of the principals would serve a prison sentence, but for a crime rather than a building violation. Pershing's booster Terry Trupp, riding the wave of antiregulatory sentiment, was elected mayor of South Lake Tahoe. In June 1989 his political career came to an abrupt, inglorious end. One of Tahoe's most infamous incidents culminated with Trupp's arrest for attempting to launder $650,000 provided by federal undercover agents. Dubbed by the FBI "Operation Deep Snow," the sting broke up a cocaine ring centered on the south shore, netting more than twenty individuals. For more than a year Trupp maintained his innocence before finally pleading guilty in August 1990 and being sentenced to nine years in prison.

The role of Trupp's Council for Logic had been usurped earlier by a group called the "Tahoe-Sierra Preservation Council" (the Preservation Council). Formed in 1980 by area property and business owners, it focused on the protection of private property rights. Even before its formation, the political battle over development at the lake had undergone a radical transformation. By the end of the 1970s it was apparent that, as constituted, the TRPA could not control traffic congestion or air and water pollution. Realizing the lake's rapid decline, powerful ninth-term U.S. representative Phillip Burton of California pushed through the Burton-Santini Act. It authorized the sale of ten thousand acres near Las Vegas and the use of the money for the purchase of environmentally sensitive lands at the lake.

The League, with the support of California congressman Vic Fazio, wanted the federal government to go further. The *Los Angeles Times* reported that those who created and nurtured the plan for a bistate agency were ready to abandon it. The TRPA, the newspaper said, was unable to plan anything except casinos and shopping centers. Referring to the TRPA, League director Jim Breuner said simply, "It failed."

Fazio introduced legislation that would create a national scenic area at Tahoe. The Forest Service would govern the basin, and all building would be restricted by a moratorium. The proposal failed but helped initiate a compromise between the states. Those who feared complete federal control now were willing to seek compromise with those who recognized the area's rapid deterioration. With some dozen sites zoned for building new casinos, the representatives of those already in existence came to the realization that gambling in such a confined area was a zero-sum game and it would be in their interests to prohibit further growth. A revised TRPA seemed the least egregious government action for all concerned.

California state senator John Garamendi and Nevada's Joe Dini met, sometimes in secret, to flesh out an agreement for a reconstituted TRPA. Frankie Sue Del Papa, who as a Nevada staff member was one of the principals involved in the process, went on to become the first woman elected Nevada's secretary of state, serving twelve years before term limits kept her from running again. In December 1980 President Jimmy Carter signed legislation that reorganized the TRPA to strengthen controls over growth and prohibit further building of gambling establishments at the lake. The new compact raised the number of at-large representatives from the states so they outnumbered those of local interests and eliminated the necessity of both states' agreeing and the sixty-day automatic approval of projects. It also required the setting of environmental thresholds and ordinances for enforcing their achievement.

In August 1982 threshold standards devised by scientists and negotiated by members of the TRPA were adopted. They were established at levels that would maintain values regarding water, soil, air, noise pollution, vegetation, and several other areas. But the problem of how they might be attained remained contentious. An ironic reversal of state roles occurred with the election of Democratic governor Richard Bryan in Nevada and Republican George Deukmejian in California. Nevada's chief executive now took steps to protect Tahoe's environment, while California's assembly Democrats were forced to file suit against the Deukmejian administration for stalling appointments to the commission that would allocate the Burton-Santini Act money. The competition of California appointments to the TRPA changed from primarily environmentalists to those who supported the interests of development.

The TRPA was again in chaos. At the end of 1982, unable to reach agreement on how to meet its adopted threshold standards, it issued a limited building moratorium to remain in place until the following August, the congressional deadline for its regional plan. When it failed to achieve consensus by August 1983, it established a second moratorium. The City of South Lake Tahoe and the Preservation Council filed suit. No one was surprised when the Associated Press described the TRPA as bitterly divided.

In November a *New York Times* headline read, "Once Pristine Lake Is Found to Be Deteriorating." Regarding tests showing a severe decline in water quality, Charles Goldman commented, "This is by far the worst we've ever recorded." He blamed construction along the shores for allowing nutrients to enter the lake. Outgoing League director Breuner called attention to a startling piece of information: "A straight line projection of the figures shows that Tahoe will become a very ordinary lake in forty years—within our lifetimes." Local government officials, on the other hand, worried about a decline in retail sales and motel occupancy rates, and they expressed outrage at the moratorium's effect on the disappearing construction industry.

Months of heated debate appeared to culminate in April 1984 when the TRPA's governing body issued its new standards and simultaneously lifted its building moratorium. The new plan included approval of six hundred new homes annually for the next three years. The day the TRPA issued its report the California attorney general filed a lawsuit against it. The next day the League filed a similar suit. The League's new director, Tom Martens, argued that the plan allowed far too much building while providing no time schedules for remedial work. In May U.S. District Judge Edward Garcia agreed, issuing an opinion that the TRPA's current course would only "contribute to the deterioration" of the lake's environmental quality. He placed a temporary restraining order on the TRPA that reinstated the ban on new construction. Several weeks later the Preservation Council filed suit from the opposing side, claiming the agency's moratoria deprived owners of their property without just compensation.

California looked to further meet its needs in the basin in 1984 by establishing the California Tahoe Conservancy. Unlike the CTRPA, the conservancy was not a regulatory agency. It proposed to use bond money to acquire sensitive sites from willing buyers to prevent damage or if necessary restore them to a former state. Its goals were to improve water quality, provide public access and recreation, and preserve wildlife habitat. Although in 2008 the financial crisis in California began seriously affecting the conservancy's programs, in the previous twenty-four years it purchased thousands of acres and met many of its goals.

In 1985 the various interest groups were split into two distinct camps. The League, the most vocal group seeking environmental protection, and the Preservation Council, representing property owners, developers, and those with economic interests, were at opposite ends of the spectrum. State and federal officials, miscellaneous citizens, and TRPA officials were generally more moderate allies of the League, while local government and business leaders and officials of local public utility districts—charged with providing day-to-day services to particular service districts—were more apt to be moderately aligned with the Preservation Council.

Scientists and researchers had been publishing findings about the deterioration of water quality since the 1960s. They had also been offering solutions, from moving sewage out of the basin to controlling the disturbance of the watershed and filtering nutrient-rich groundwater. Unsurprisingly, a study by the Georgia Institute of Technology found that stakeholders in favor of environmental protections expressed confidence in the scientists, while stakeholders who favored growth were more likely to distrust them.

Each side questioned the goals and interests, as well as the legitimacy of the motives, of the other side. Typical of comments from the environmental coalition was that the Preservation Council's goals were to "build, build, and build more." League members believed that while ostensibly looking out for the small property owner, the Preservation Council was actually a shill for the real estate and construction industries. The economic growth faction accused the League of being composed of either overzealous environmentalists—one called them the "squirrel and pinenut crowd"—or "fat cats" who wished "to pull up the gangplank now that they each have their Tahoe place." Each side believed the other was resorting to unscrupulous measures, and the acrimony caused the conflict to intensify.

At the time western states were heavily influenced by the "Sagebrush Rebellion," wherein state politicians, backed by mining corporations, oil interests, loggers, developers, and ranchers, sought to take control of federal lands. Several years earlier the Nevada legislature had filed suit in a failed attempt to claim for the state nearly fifty million acres of federally managed lands. An avowed Sagebrush advocate, President Ronald Reagan cut spending on research for energy conservation and renewable energy resources but, with limited congressional support, did not push the idea that public domain truly belonged to the states. With their "Sagebrush" options dwindling, the last thing frustrated Nevada lawmakers wanted was more federal intervention at the lake. Furthermore, they strongly resented that the bistate TRPA had come under the control of a judge from California, albeit a U.S. District Court judge.

Throughout 1984 and into 1985 the Preservation Council lobbied the Nevada legislature to simply withdraw from the bistate compact. On March 10, 1985, a *New York Times* headline read, "Irate Property Owners Fuel Attack on Tahoe Planning Agency." That same day the Nevada General Assembly passed and sent to the senate a bill to terminate Nevada's participation in the TRPA. Governor Bryan said he would veto the bill if it came to his desk. The bill was withdrawn a few weeks later, but it added to the hardening positions of the warring factions.

On April 1, 1985, Bill Morgan took over what seemed an impossible position: executive director of the TRPA. Morgan left his position as the supervisor for the U.S. Forest Service at Tahoe to accept the post. He had directed the Tahoe forest agency for ten years, three years of which he had been the federal representative on the TRPA executive board. His calm demeanor and measured approach to problems had earned him the respect of both fractious camps. Once selected, after getting a sense of direction by talking to each TRPA representative, Morgan spent time convincing the Nevada legislature to give the agency one more chance. He offered them veto power over any agreement that might be forged.

At a large public meeting he made a popular decision by rejecting a proposed settlement agreement with the California Attorney General's Office and the League, believing it went too far in regulating land use. At another meeting, public feelings were roused when misinformation was spread that the Forest Service intended to condemn properties in order to seize them. Morgan stepped before the unfriendly crowd and reminded it that the agency had never condemned land at the lake. He also pointed out that the government's mandate included the stipulation that any transaction must involve a "willing seller" as well as a will-

In 1985 Bill Morgan gave up his position as the U.S. Forest Service Lake Tahoe supervisor to take the impossible and thankless job as TRPA director. (Courtesy Carole Morgan)

ing buyer. His message, delivered in his usual soft-spoken manner, tempered the ill feelings.

In his tenure with the Forest Service, Morgan had been trained in conciliation and reaching consensus, and he had facilitated groups dealing with difficult issues within the agency. He now proposed that in lieu of continuing the formal, generally unproductive meetings, representatives of all stakeholders should come together for attempts at consensus building.

In July 1985 the Ninth Circuit Court of Appeals gave the environmental forces a victory when it upheld the lower court's moratorium, finding "convincing evidence" that unless action reversed current trends, most of the lake's clarity would be lost within forty years. The pronouncement made it apparent that there would be no further building without an agreement between the stakeholders ratified by the states and the TRPA. That determination pushed the factions to take part in Morgan's improbable stratagem. Hostility and deeply entrenched positions notwithstanding, representatives from thirty interest groups were enlisted to attend consensus-building workshops.

Participants met under the direction of an outside facilitator over the course of ten months for two-day meetings, one to three times a month. Once they began talking directly to one another, and realized that the needs and interests of all parties were going to be considered, stereotypes gave way to more nuanced viewpoints and misperceptions were dispelled. The League, represented by its new director, Tom Martens, demonstrated that it was not trying to prohibit all building, and the Preservation Council, led by attorney Larry Hoffman, showed it would support a broad range of efforts, including various land-acquisition programs.

The facilitator noted one of the early signs of transformation when a member of the environmental group offered coffee to one of the individuals from the property-rights group. Still, there were heated arguments and junctures at which opposing parties had to be coaxed back to the table. At Morgan's direction, as the groups worked together, the facilitator intervened less and less. In the end, one member said that negative feelings were channeled into positive solutions.

In June 1986 the consensus group produced a final document. Most of the concerns of the key stakeholders had been met. Compromises led to planning for two thousand new residences to be approved between 1986 and 1991, as well as four hundred thousand square feet of commercial buildings over the next ten years. A bond issue in California had designated eighty-four million dollars for acquiring sensitive land on the California side of the basin. In November 1986 Nevadans passed a thirty-one-million-dollar bond issue to purchase Nevada lots unsuitable for building.

Despite the progress, feelings among TRPA members remained intense. It took a year of negotiations to incorporate the consensus group's ideas into a new TRPA Master Plan. The agency finally ratified the plan on June 4, 1987. A Deukmejian appointee commented that he strongly objected to much of the plan, and if it had not been tied to the dismissal of the building moratorium, he would not have considered voting for it. The Nevada Senate now took its turn at passing a bill to pull the state out of the bistate agency. Its bill would take effect unless the lawsuit prohibiting building was lifted by September 1. Governor Bryan again vowed to veto any TRPA pullout legislation, and with an agreement seemingly at hand, the lawmakers did not pursue the threat.

California's Deukmejian, running for reelection, toured the lake and now pledged to work for its preservation. Thereafter, his office backed full appropriations for the TRPA and bond funds for lot purchases. The action came just in time, as the Reagan administration cut fourteen million dollars from the federal government's commitment. In 1987 money from California bonds would purchase as many as one thousand lots.

With the TRPA Master Plan approved, on July 16, 1987, U.S. District Court Judge Garcia dismissed the lawsuit, ending the moratorium. "The judge can now bow out," he said. His action gave the economically depressed area its first building season in four years.

As for the Preservation Council's lawsuit against the TRPA, it wound its way through the court system until it was heard by the U.S. Supreme Court in 2002. The Preservation Council argued that the TRPA's denial of individuals' uses of their lands required market-value compensation. The moratoria, they claimed, consisted of takings—that is, property taken for public use—as described by the "Takings Clause" in the Fifth and Fourteenth amendments.

In the argument's first test, the district court found in favor of the Preservation Council, since owners had been deprived of any economic use of their lands during the moratoria. The Ninth Circuit Court of Appeals reversed the decision, finding that since the moratoria had only temporary impacts, no taking occurred. Future chief justice John Roberts argued the case for the TRPA in the Supreme Court. In an extensively analyzed decision, it found there was an inherent difference between the *acquisition* of property for public use and the *regulation* of property *from* public use. Hence, no compensation was required. Actions that would lead to another court dispute began sometime around 1988. This battle would be waged over the Washoe Indians' sacred place, Cave Rock, and would take almost twenty years to be resolved.

Chapter Eleven

The Battle for Cave Rock

*M*any Washoe Indians believe Cave Rock is so sacrosanct that to get to nearby destinations, they will follow the winding highway seventy-two miles around the lake rather than drive through its tunnels. When sport rock climbers discovered the massif, they were unaware of the importance of the site to the Indians and began setting anchors in the granite to develop routes. After a couple of years of use, the formation became a world-class climbing site and soon had the highest concentration of difficult sport climbs at Lake Tahoe. While Washoes regarded it as a cultural shrine, the *San Francisco Chronicle* described it as "a [climbers] refuge with the most gymnastic routes in the state." The complexities presented by the rock's overhang and steep walls, the quality of the routes, the ease of access, and the aesthetic qualities of the setting earned it an international reputation. But, as one climbing guidebook described it, the face of Cave Rock began to resemble "a grid of bolts."

When Nevada officials proposed an expansion of the boat ramp below Cave Rock in 1992, the Washoe Tribal Council notified them of the property's sacred status. In reviewing the boating project (which the tribe would fight against and lose), Brian Wallace, newly elected Washoe tribal chair, became aware of the climbing apparatus in the rock. He responded to a Tahoe Regional Planning Agency query by saying, "We believe the most recent destruction of the Cave Rock site . . . adds insult to injury in the disturbing recent history of this very religious place."

Cave Rock, "De' ek wadapush" in Washoe, is the 360-foot core remnant of a volcano that erupted three million years ago. (Courtesy Special Collections, University of Nevada, Reno, Library)

As more became known, tribal elders expressed offense at what they considered physical desecration of the site as well as the names of many routes. The more egregious included "Cave Man," "Super Monkey," "Trash Dog," "Bat Out of Hell," and "Shut the Fuck Up and Climb."

Climbers reacted in various ways to Washoe concerns. One route developer argued that climbers had cleaned up "a rubble heap . . . left over from when tunnels were blasted through Cave Rock." He continued, "I think the tunnel itself took away any sacred value of the place."

Another builder, Dimitri Barton, took the opposite view. Calling it a "very, very special place" that he would hate to see off-limits, he said he would stop climbing there to honor Washoe wishes. He added the comment that the tribe had been "screwed enough" throughout history.

Other climbers who used the site agreed with a Reno man who said, "We don't want to be an enemy to anybody. We just want to compromise and coexist. Everybody should have a chance to enjoy it." Tribal chair Wallace worried that recent publicity would encourage further destruction. He insisted that "a religious object of extreme significance is increasingly endangered." He announced, "Officials of the Washoe Indian Tribe hope to ban rock climbing at Cave Rock."

Startled by the Washoe leader's statements, several climbers contacted the Access Fund, a Boulder, Colorado–based advocacy group. Its stated mission emphasizes its priorities to keep climbing in public areas open and support climbers' constitutional rights. The Access Fund supported the climbers against the Washoes, bringing ample resources to the dispute. Begun in 1989, it had more than seventy organizations contributing financial support in the mid-'90s, including Nike, Microsoft, Charles Schwab, North Face, and REI. Yearly corporate contributions to the group, at that time, ranged up to and over $20,000 per organization. By the time the Cave Rock dispute would be settled, the Access Fund was raising well over $1 million a year—$1,245,583 in 2007, with more than $300,000 coming from corporate sponsorships and grants.

The climbers declared that because the rock was on public land, they had the right to use it. A climbing prohibition, they said, would violate the multiple-use policy for federal lands. They also argued that the highway tunnels blown through the lower portion of the rock and the noise of traffic irreparably damaged the site as a cultural property. The Washoe Tribal Council protested the scarring of the rock and the sustained human contact with it that climbing fostered. They demanded that the activity stop and the anchors be removed.

The history of Washoes and Cave Rock revolved around the tribe's shamans. They used the site for many hundreds of years and when the Americans arrived, both before and after the tunnels were built. Shamanic power came to an individual unsought in visions or dreams. Once developed, it might be used for curing sickness or for witchcraft, such as "shooting" a foreign body into an adversary. Those who ignored the calling of power or who foolishly attempted to seek it of their own volition placed themselves in mortal danger.

The most renowned of the shamans was Henry Rupert, who lived in the Carson Valley until his death in 1965. He used his shamanic power for healing only, and his fame and influence as a healer crossed cultural boundaries. He even cured a white Protestant minister in Carson City who suffered from migraine headaches that American doctors could not effectively treat. Rupert believed healing involved individual perception and "psychological set." He used hypnosis, incantations, and magical displays to win patients' confidence in his curative skills. The "doctoring" of the minister involved a bit of legerdemain, or sleight of hand, that produced a pencil, symbolizing that the minister was working too hard.

Rupert, like other Washoe healers, used secret rites at Cave Rock to

Henry Rupert, the most renowned of the Washoe Indian shamans. *Detail.* (Courtesy Special Collections, University of Nevada, Reno, Library)

tap into a spiritual dimension and increase his shamanic powers. He would not talk about the rituals or powers other than in general terms. He believed all beings contained energy, and his cosmology centered on "ethereal waves," likened to "electric waves or pulses of energy." In the spirit world, he believed, energy came from a pure layer where the Creator, or omnipotent being, exists. The essence of power from that layer facilitated all his healing.

Rupert knew that his shamanism appeared strange to the uninitiated, telling an anthropologist, "You don't know what I am talking about, and the same is true for anybody who reads this thing you write. What is real for me is not real for you."

Among the many Native and non-Native individuals recorded as being healed by Rupert were a Mexican woman in Sacramento diagnosed by doctors as having a malignant tumor of the abdomen, a World War II veteran whose hallucinations that German soldiers were trying to strangle him with barbed wire caused him to lacerate his own neck, and a white storekeeper with heart problems. The storekeeper, who lived seventy-five miles away, in Fallon, Nevada, claimed he would never again see a doctor other than Rupert. Although Rupert was the last publicly active Washoe shaman to use Cave Rock, the site remains a place of extreme power to Washoes, and modern practitioners continue to visit it.

Because of the dispute over the rock's use, in the 1990s the Forest Service evaluated its historical value. In 1996, because of its long association with the Washoes, Cave Rock gained eligibility for inclusion on the National Register of Historic Places as a Traditional Cultural Property. In February 1997 Robert Harris, the U.S. Forest Service supervisor for Lake Tahoe, imposed a temporary closure order, forbidding climbing on the rock in order to study the issue. Three months later, in May, when Harris retired, Juan Palma, the new supervisor, lifted the ban.

In 1998 the keeper of the National Register found that Cave Rock was also eligible for designation as a National Historic Transportation District and an archaeological site. These findings added to its stature as a Traditional Cultural Property. At the same time, it had been determined that rock climbing posed an ongoing adverse effect to the site's integrity. The criteria for an adverse effect included physical destruction, damage, or alteration of the property's character. By then the cave hosted a steady stream of sport climbers from around the world. Part of its floor was paved, and some 325 anchors marked forty-seven distinct technical routes on the rock face. The Forest Service began attempts to mediate between the Washoes and the climbers. Its attempts were doomed from the start. It sought concessions from both Washoes and climbers. Tribal chair Wallace consistently stated that the tribe's sole concern was the integrity of the site and that damage resulted from *any* unauthorized human presence. For Washoes, the matter was nonnegotiable.

On January 13, 1999, forest supervisor Palma issued his decision for a preferred alternative. He explained that he had attempted to strike a balance between all those who considered Cave Rock important while protecting the Traditional Cultural Property. The proposal stated, "Public Access, including rock climbing, is allowed . . . and will be managed to minimize conflicts and impacts."

The Washoes were grievously disappointed and immediately protested the proposal. They were joined by a host of individuals and orga-

This photo, circa 1865, helps illustrate Cave Rock's eligibility for designation as a National Historic Transportation District. (Courtesy Special Collections, University of Nevada, Reno, Library)

nizations, including the National Advisory Council on Historic Preservation and the Nevada State Historic Preservation Office. Former forest supervisor Harris stated that the proposed alternative did not fully comply with laws protecting heritage resources. He asked how an alternative that had significant environmental impacts upon heritage resources could be selected.

There was one paramount problem with Palma's preferred alternative that had been recognized by at least three entities—the Advisory Council on Historic Protection, tribal chair Wallace, and former supervisor Harris: The selection of the alternative did not follow the standards and guidelines of the Lake Tahoe Basin Management Unit's own Forest Plan. The plan included a priority listing of resources to be used in resolving conflicts. Nine items ranked in order can be summarized:

1. protection of water quality in Lake Tahoe
2. protection of threatened or endangered species
3. preservation of significant cultural resources
4. achievement of air-quality standards
5. maintenance of viable populations of wildlife
6. achievement of diverse vegetation communities
7. establishment of outdoor recreation facilities and uses
8. harvesting and treatment of timber stands
9. utilization of grazing forage

The fact that the item mandating protection of cultural resources was third on the list and recreation four places below had obviously not been used in making the decision. Tribal chair Wallace called attention to the fact that to disregard the rankings deviated from the Forest Plan. The Advisory Council pointed out that there seemed no justification for diverging from the ranking system. Former supervisor Harris stated that it was "of utmost importance" that the public be told why the Forest Plan had not been followed. These observations would not be answered by supervisor Palma. He had taken a job as a Bureau of Land Management ranger in Oregon.

Maribeth Gustafson, a nineteen-year career Forest Service employee, became supervisor of the Lake Tahoe Basin Management Unit in July 2000. When she arrived at Lake Tahoe she visited Cave Rock with Forest

Service archaeologist John Maher. He had taken Palma to the site three years earlier, explaining the intricacies of the issues. He now gave Gustafson a similar presentation. She studied the issue, interviewed the principals, and came up with a decidedly different alternative. She proposed eliminating climbing to provide maximum protection of the resource.

The new decision would allow activities consistent with the historic period at Cave Rock, defined as prehistoric times through 1965. She selected 1965 because Henry Rupert died that year. Rupert's association with the rock had contributed significantly to its National Register eligibility. Gustafson noted that his influence crossed cultural and ethnic boundaries and that he adapted his healing to the changing world, exemplifying "the tension Native traditional practitioners maintain between tradition, experimentation, and innovation." According to the Gustafson alternative, Cave Rock would be managed to protect its status as a Traditional Cultural Property, and anything adversely affecting that would be prohibited.

The Access Fund immediately filed suit. The case, cited as *Access Fund v. U.S. Department of Agriculture,* took the battle to the federal courts. In previous court cases like Cave Rock, the Native litigants had lost. Prior to the last decade of the twentieth century, no Native American sacred-site claim had ever been upheld in a federal court. Whereas the Catholic missions gained protection and other religious sites are national monuments, including the National Cathedral in Washington, D.C., the Touro Synagogue, and the Sixteenth Street Baptist Church in Birmingham, Alabama, Native sites continued to be exploited, developed, and destroyed.

In its suit the Access Fund declared that because Cave Rock is a religious site, protecting it violates the First Amendment's Establishment Clause: "Congress shall make no law respecting an establishment of religion, or prohibiting the free exercise thereof." The group charged that the Forest Service labeled it a cultural property merely to evade legal challenges. "Listing Cave Rock as a traditional cultural property does not change the fundamental nature of Cave Rock as a religious site," the complaint argued. Gustafson dismissed the charge: "Some have characterized this issue as a Native American religion versus climber conflict, yet this is simply not the case," she said. "Rather the decision is actually based on resource values versus user impacts. . . . The significant historic, cultural, and scientific values present at Cave Rock are deserving of maximum protection."

Climbing continued at the site because the court did not hear the case until January 28, 2005, a year and a half after the Gustafson decision. When ruling, the U.S. District Court judge in Reno stated that he would not necessarily have made the same decision as the forest supervisor, but he rejected the Access Fund's contentions. Since the supervisor had observed all applicable laws and followed her agency's policies, he found no reason to annul her decision. He found in favor of the Forest Service as regarded contentions concerning the First Amendment, and he upheld the climbing ban.

The Access Fund directors were worried that hundreds of public-land units might be similarly affected if it allowed a legal precedent to be established. On March 22, 2005, calling the ban "unreasonable and unnecessary," the Access Fund announced it would appeal the decision to the Ninth Circuit Court of Appeals.

The Ninth Circuit Court also disagreed with the Access Fund's position. It noted that the Forest Service consistently stated, and presented thorough documentation showing, that secular purpose motivated the protection of Cave Rock as a cultural, historical, and archaeological monument. The agency had decided that although the property may at times be discussed in religious terms, its significance was based not on Washoe religious doctrine but on the historic and ethnographic record. On August 27, 2007, it upheld the U.S. District Court's ruling, and rock climbing at the sacred monolith ended.

With the last decision, the climbing group gave up its legal challenge. The case set a precedent: For the first time, Native American concerns caused the involuntary closure of a climbing site on federal property.

John Dayberry, an educator and conservationist with a California contractor's license, assisted by his son Christian and friend Bill Atkins, undertook the difficult job of removing the anchors from the rock and the cement and paving stones from the cave floor. The process of working on the rock face was dangerous. Dangling at the end of a rope in a bosun's chair, similar to a climbing harness with a rigid seat, the elder Dayberry had to secure himself to a set anchor and jam a temporary

cam or nut into a crevice. He then moved the rope from the anchor to the temporary device. After pulling out each bolt and sleeve and plugging and cementing the hole, he held himself with a hand jam in the crevice, removed the cam, and let go. The fall could be up to twelve feet, depending on the location of the next bolt. Once a piece of rock above him broke off, crashing against Dayberry's hard hat and glancing off his shoulder. Another time, after Dayberry finished work, a four-hundred-pound boulder broke free and fell to the cave floor. Had it broken free while he was working, it would have taken him with it.

In the spring of 2009, with the cave restored to its original appearance, John Dayberry made two interesting comments. He said that 80 percent of the climbers he encountered were happy for the tribe, saying, "Most feel it's the least we could do for them." He also noted that flaking on the rock face had destabilized many of the bolts, and there had been water behind bolts in the cave ceiling. He said, "Sooner or later they all would have failed." With Cave Rock still under the jurisdiction of the Forest Service, the Washoe Indians had regained their sacred site, and the integrity of a valuable cultural resource at the lake had been reestablished.

Chapter Twelve

The Daring

$\mathcal{D}$an Osman was the climber most identified with Cave Rock. He used the site to hone his climbing skills while building a number of routes. By 1992 he had created four of the site's seven highest-rated routes and soon achieved extreme sport-superstar status.

Osman's climbing feats became legendary. He was filmed doing numerous daredevil climbs: free soloing (climbing without any safety apparatus) up a sheer rock face where a misstep would mean death, leaping to catch a crack at the top of a route, and hurdling to a narrow crag across a deep abyss.

For any climber, falling and being caught by the safety rope is an integral part of the sport. Building one of his limit-pushing routes, Osman, while searching for hand placements in the overhanging rock, fell time after time—perhaps fifty falls attempting to set one bolt. Although secured by his rope, each fall caused a jolt of fear. Osman eventually concluded that falling, not climbing, was the ultimate thrill. At Cave Rock he began studying and practicing falling while tethered with the rope. He soon began making adventure videos and MTV commercials of his single-rope jumps from other rocks, bridges, and cliffs. Osman's plunges got progressively longer: 50 feet, 250 feet, and eventually 1,000 feet. While making the extreme sport videos, he secured contracts to test ropes and rigging for companies that manufactured climbing gear.

In October 1998, at age thirty-five, Osman traveled to Yosemite Valley to attempt a record jump from the rock named Leaning Tower. After a week doing jumps that eventually reached 900 feet, he got a call from his young daughter in Carson Valley. She wanted to see him, so, leaving the rigged ropes in place, he returned home. Driving back to the park, he was stopped by authorities and jailed for unpaid vehicle citations. It was not until late in the afternoon of November 23 that he finally managed to again use the setup. Darkness was setting in as he added rope so he could jump using more than 1,000 feet of line. The additional length changed the angle of the jump and placed undue pressure on one of the knots. He jumped, the line snapped, and Osman fell to his death. Five days later, more than two hundred friends gathered as his ashes were spread over Lake Tahoe at Cave Rock.

Another of Tahoe's extreme sport superstars suffered a tragic death at a young age. Steve McKinney died at thirty-six years old while sleeping in an automobile pulled off to the side of a California highway. In November 1990 a drunk driver crashed into the back of McKinney's car, killing him in his sleep. The irony in the tragedy is implicit in a description by his friend Craig Calonica, from South Shore. Calonica, who represented the United States in speed skiing from 1974 to 1987 and later became a pioneer skier in Nepal's Himalayas, tells of McKinney's surviving helicopter crashes, hang-glider crashes, speed-racing crashes, and a climbing fall that broke his back, yet always coming back to "pull off the unbelievable again."

McKinney, at age twenty in 1973, walked away from a position as a downhill racer for the U.S. Ski Team, calling the politicians running the team "air brained." Invited to the World Cup races at Heavenly Valley, he said, "Instead I got stoned, and the day of the races hitchhiked to San Francisco and caught a boat to Alaska." After three weeks of "working with fish in the rain," he returned to California to become a rock climber and speed skier. An incident on 24,785-foot Mustagh Ata in China allows insight into his character. After a particularly strenuous climb to the summit, he turned around and did it again to help a double amputee accomplish his goal of reaching the peak.

McKinney was dubbed the "high priest of speed skiing." Going straight down radical one-mile runs, speed skiing is the fastest non-motorized sport on earth and has been deemed too dangerous for the

Olympic Games. McKinney set five world speed-skiing records, the last at 124.762 mph. He was also the first person to hang glide off Mount Everest. Other activities included mountaineer skiing around the lake before a Tahoe Rim Trail existed, big-wall climbing—multipitch climbs that generally require more than one day—and mountain climbing in the Himalayas. When asked how he could risk skiing bare-handed down a treacherous slope, he said that "falling wasn't something he had planned on his run." Dick Dorworth, a renowned speed skier and ski historian, described McKinney as a magnetic personality and the most important speed skier who ever lived. Dorworth commented further, "In my mind Steve McKinney was a great speed skier because he was a great human being, not vice-versa."

Time called Tamara McKinney, Steve's younger sister, "America's queen of the hill." The entire family skied, as their divorced mother, working as a ski instructor at Mount Rose, raised seven children. Five of the seven reached the U.S. Ski Team. Tamara, the youngest child, remembers being young and Steve "screaming" downhill, holding her on his back with one hand. During her ski career she represented the United States in three Olympics and, in 1983, became the first American woman to win the overall World Cup title. In all, Tamara McKinney won nine national titles and eighteen World Cup races, nine in slalom and nine in giant slalom. She persevered through a series of injuries, including competing in the 1988 Olympics on a broken leg. In 1989 she retired from World Cup racing when she broke her leg in ten places. Yet she returned to race professionally, winning the Tournament of Champions four years later. In the 1990s Tamara McKinney, who continues to live in Squaw Valley and coaches the junior racing team, became a spokesperson for the Jimmie Heuga foundation Can Do Multiple Sclerosis, begun by Heuga, another of Tahoe's and America's skiing greats.

Heuga, who died at age sixty-six in February 2010 of complications from multiple sclerosis (MS), is a legend in American skiing. Born in Tahoe City, he grew up in Squaw Valley, where his Basque immigrant father ran the resort's cable car. At age fifteen, in 1958, he became the youngest person ever to make the U.S. Men's Ski Team. At the 1964 Olympic Games in Innsbruck, Austria, the American men's alpine team was being shut out of the medal count, which was typical; no American had ever medaled in an Olympic alpine event. Not only that, but in Innsbruck they were being treated with disrespect. The night before the slalom, a security guard had bullied Heuga, who at age twenty stood five-foot-six and weighed 140 pounds, pushing him around. But what a race the slalom was for the American men. Heuga finished third; his teammate and good friend Billy Kidd finished second. Kidd described the outcome: "I missed the gold medal by 14 hundredths of a second. So blink your eye. That's 14 hundredths of a second. And Jimmie was another blink behind." If only one of the team members had medaled, it might have been considered luck; with both taking the podium, it showed that the Americans had arrived. That night the guard who had roughed up Heuga ushered him to the victory stand.

In his next Olympic appearance, in 1968, despite two top-ten finishes, Heuga could not gain proper timing. He felt listless and tired. It turned out to be the beginning stages of MS. His Hall of Fame skiing career ended, and doctors told him to cease all physical activity, the common treatment for the incurable disease. Instead, Heuga decided to live his life as fully as he could. For the next forty years he followed a strict, goal-oriented exercise regimen and participated in "active living," including sit-skiing. He lived his mantra: "Do the best with what you have." He founded his wellness center, helping others fight MS. "I'm the least qualified person to found a medical center," Heuga said, "but I do know how to live. You just can't wait for the lights to be shut off." His legacy is reflected in the fact that the holistic treatment of MS patients now routinely includes physical therapy and strengthening exercises.

In eulogizing Heuga, a common theme emerged from those who knew him best. Kidd said, "Jimmie's accomplishments on the race course will forever be remembered. But it's his accomplishments and drive in the fight against MS that will continue to help so many people live their lives. His life is an inspiration." Leif Grevle, a longtime friend and member of the 1964 Norway Ski Team, said, "His generosity, giving so much to everyone else even though he had that dreadful disease, is, to me, unbelievable." U.S. Ski Team president Bill Marolt, who skied with Heuga on the 1964 team, summarized what many felt: "Jimmie Heuga was a champion in every sense of the word."

Another Tahoe athlete whose charisma has been a boon to the sport

Glen Plake, in a 1988 Bumps Competition at Heavenly Valley, before developing his trademark Mohawk hairstyle. (Courtesy *Tahoe Daily Tribune* Archive)

of skiing is Heavenly Valley's Glen Plake. Starring in numerous ski movies with his multicolored Mohawk haircut, by the turn of the twenty-first century he was the most recognizable skier in the world. The freestyler's energy and enthusiasm were contagious, and his showmanship on the slopes was unprecedented. A three-time winner of the World Hot Dog Championship who epitomized the fun and joy of skiing, in 2010 he was inducted into the U.S. Ski and Snowboard Hall of Fame.

Plake's South Shore friend Shaun Palmer has been named by various publications Athlete of the Year, Extreme Athlete of the Year, and Action Athlete of the Year. *USA Today* newspaper once acclaimed Palmer as the World's Greatest Athlete. He was a snowboarding pioneer and one of the founding fathers of extreme sports. He and Plake invented snowboard cross—where competitors race side by side. Palmer's gold-medal record in various speed and extreme sports is unmatched. In the Winter X Games, between 1997, when the Games began, and 2001, he captured at least one gold medal each year. As only he could, the medals were earned in four different events: snow mountain-bike racing, snowboard cross, ski cross, and in 2001 ultra cross, a relay with fellow South Tahoe skier Chris Hernandez.

As a preteen and teen, Palmer could be seen in South Tahoe, but only if you looked fast and in someplace other than school. He was always riding a bike or a skateboard, doing stunts. He built his first snowboard when he was twelve years old, in 1980, and taught himself to ride. Snowboarding was in its infancy, and the major ski resorts prohibited boards on their slopes. That prohibition probably helped attract Palmer, who would climb hills to board down and "just figure out what felt right." Three years after beginning to snowboard, he quit high school to take part in a fledgling junior snowboarding tour. He quickly became junior world champion and defended his title for the next few years. Palmer's mother said, "Whether it was on wheels or on a board, it had to be superfast—he had no fear."

At age twenty Palmer won the World Snowboarding Championship and defended his title the following year. In 1995, at twenty-six, he began learning to race on a mountain bike from veteran bikers. He quickly mastered their techniques, and a year later he won the downhill at North America's premier off-road race, the NORBA National Mountain Bike Championships. At the end of that season he ranked number five in the World Cup rankings. In 1997 a national sponsor signed Palmer to the largest contract ever assigned a mountain biker, three hundred thousand dollars annually. In 2003 he said he had gotten all the speed he could from gravity and thought to try a motorcycle. In his first professional race, at the Los Angeles Coliseum, he performed the unheard-of feat of qualifying for the 125cc Supercross main event. In 2006, at age thirty-seven, Palmer qualified for the U.S. Olympic Snowboard Team, only to rip his Achilles' tendon in half two weeks before the Games' opening.

Success for Palmer did not come without cost. Throughout his career, along with his athleticism, he earned the reputation of a world-class partyer. One night in 2005, after a falling-out with sponsors, he fell into an alcohol- and drug-induced coma and was taken by a CareFlight helicopter to a Reno hospital. After completing a rehab program, he said, "I definitely have an addictive personality. Everything I do is full throttle. As far as winning . . . I'm addicted to this too, but it's a healthy one. That's why I'm trying to stick it out." Turning to a new sport in 2008, he won the Jeep King of the Mountain overall championship.

After thirteen years and three Olympics,

Shaun Palmer, once acclaimed by *USA Today* as the World's Greatest Athlete. (Courtesy budfawcett.com)

Daron Rahlves, of Truckee, had become the most successful men's down-hiller in U.S. Alpine Ski Team history. He amassed twelve World Cup victories and twenty-eight podiums before retiring, only to come back to compete in ski-cross events. Ski cross is described as roller derby on skis, with four to six racers competing alongside one another, going over jumps and bumps in roller-coaster fashion. After winning gold in the 2008 Winter X Games ski cross, Rahlves dislocated his hip for the fourth time while preparing for the 2010 Olympics. Three weeks after leaving the hospital, he competed at the Vancouver Olympics, saying, "It comes down to charging from the get-go." A collision and crash in a qualifying run pushed him into his second retirement. In October 2010 Rahlves was named as an inductee into the U.S. Ski and Snowboard Hall of Fame.

There are several other world champion competitors among the many outstanding Tahoe skiers competing in the first decades of the twenty-first century. Freestyler Shannon Bahrke grew up in Tahoe City. She won a silver medal in the 2006 Olympics and a bronze in 2010 to become the first American woman freestyler to win multiple medals. Over her career she accumulated twenty-two World Cup podiums and was the World Cup champion in 2003. Marco Sullivan, former North Tahoe High School football team captain, served as the U.S. Team's downhill captain in the 2010 Olympics. Sullivan, who at three years old began skiing down a gravel hill in his Tahoe backyard, has competed in three Olympic Games, and is a four-time national champion. Snowboarder Elena Hight, of South Lake Tahoe, at sixteen was the youngest woman snowboarder to compete in the 2006 Olympics and again represented the United States in the 2010 Vancouver Olympics. In between she won the bronze medal in the Winter X Games superpipe. Errol Kerr was born and raised in Truckee. He trains at Alpine Meadows. His father is Jamaican, his mother American. He skied as a downhiller on the U.S. Team before turning to the ski cross and becoming not just part of but the entire Jamaican National Ski Team for the 2010 Olympics. His ninth-place ski-cross finish in the Vancouver Games was the highest ever for a Caribbean competitor in Winter Olympics.

Squaw Valley alpine skier Julia Mancuso became the American star of the 2010 Olympics, winning silver medals in both the downhill and the combined. She had earned the gold medal in the 2006 Olympics' giant slalom, the first Tahoe skier to ever win Olympic gold, and it was done while she suffered from hip dysplasia. Her Vail surgeon could not believe she skied with such a painful injury. It required surgery and intensive rehabilitation, leading to Mancuso's breakout World Cup season in 2007. She concluded the year in third place overall, the best finish for an American woman since Tamara McKinney in 1984. Mancuso had overcome obstacles before. She began skiing at age two and racing at five. That was the same year her mother took her out to breakfast one morning so she would not see her father taken to jail.

In the late 1960s Julia's father, Ciro Mancuso, had been an outstanding ski racer at Tahoe College in Meyers, the predecessor to Sierra Nevada College at Incline Village. He went on to become a successful developer and contractor and an even more successful marijuana smuggler. For many years he masterminded an empire that brought some forty-five tons of pot, worth a reported ninety-eight million dollars, to the West Coast. After more than a decade of legal wrangling, and five and a half years in jail, he returned to Squaw Valley and reclaimed his life. He turned toxic land in Truckee into an industrial park that offers reasonable rents and developed an adjoining site into affordable housing. He also reestablished ties with Julia and his other two daughters. Julia said, "I missed my dad. . . . Maybe it had an effect on me. I turned to skiing." Growing up in the Squaw Valley racing program, she captured a U.S. record eight Junior World Championship medals, including five golds.

Julia Mancuso, the American star of the 2010 Olympics. (Courtesy Jen Desmond/USSA)

Her junior success was a harbinger for what has followed. Her three Olympic medals are the most ever for a female American alpine skier. A run at Squaw Valley is named Julia's Gold.

In March 2010 a sponsor donated ten thousand dollars to the Tahoe Truckee school district in Julia Mancuso's name. In presenting the gift, Mancuso acknowledged that her accomplishments are in large part due to growing up in the region. Thanking Mancuso, the Truckee school board president commented, "It is exciting to have so many world-class athletes in our midst. Our children are fortunate indeed to be able to grow up with these hometown heroes and their successes as real-life examples of willpower and dedication. It's a unique aspect of our community that has helped to produce so many Olympians." Youth skiing, boarding, and racing programs; club teams; high school teams; and academies located at resorts throughout the area seemingly ensure the continuation of the legacy.

Chapter Thirteen

Shaping the Gem

*I*n his "Living Waters" homily in 1863, Thomas Starr King spoke of the color of Lake Tahoe: "Hues cannot be more sharply contrasted than are these permanent colors. They do not shade into each other; they lie as clearly defined as the course of glowing gems in the wall of the New Jerusalem." Ten years later, when John LeConte visited, he referred to a "genuine childlike awe and wonder" inspired by the lake, which he called "the largest of the 'Gems of the Sierra.'" References to the lake as a gem or descriptions of its gemlike qualities are fitting. It is beautiful and continually shaped by nature or, in recent times, by man.

A dramatic example of nature's unforgiving power took place at Alpine Meadows in the spring of 1982. The ski resort's high valley floor (6,835 feet), surrounded on three sides by steep mountains, guarantees abundant, deep snow, and almost all its runs allow spectacular views of Lake Tahoe. But the resort is one of North America's few ski areas classified as an "A"-level avalanche area. There are some three hundred avalanche paths within its bounds. From its inception, the resort has utilized ski patrollers tossing hand charges, military howitzers, and avalaunchers to induce small avalanches that prevent buildups that lead to large ones.

In the spring of 1982 snow had been plentiful. Early March was warm, with the snow melting during the day and freezing again at night. At the end of March the weather changed, and snow fell for four days at a record rate. The storms buried what had been an icy crust beneath seven feet of

An avalanche at Alpine Meadows, where in 1982 three avalanches moved simultaneously to create the deadliest slide ever at a North American ski resort. (Courtesy Jim Plehn)

new snow. With the storm intensifying, the resort closed midafternoon on March 30. The next morning snow continued, and winds reached ninety miles per hour; mountain manager Bernie Kingery kept the resort shut down. Plows were working, and the road and parking lot were closed and then reopened. Ski patrollers fought the elements to detonate slides on the potential avalanche chutes. Some of their charges caused disturbingly large slab avalanches, with cohesive plates of snow breaking and falling straight downslope. The fact that the patrollers observed rubble on the road below the runs after artillery fire was a positive sign of stability, but the feeling below their feet was decidedly negative. One described the snow as "alive, truly alive." Another compared it to "standing on top of a monster." By noon on March 31, Kingery ordered the majority of employees to go home, including most of the exhausted patrollers. In the base lodge, the maintenance building, and the Summit Chair Bottom Terminal Building, a number of employees remained behind working.

At 3:45 in the afternoon everybody's favorite employee, Jake Smith, a happy-go-lucky trail crewman, on a snowmobile in the parking lot, began shouting into his radio. All that could be made out through garbled static was "Avalanche!" Five seconds later a shock wave struck the Summit Terminal Building. It preceded a shrieking, hurricane-strength wind that blasted out windows. A thirty-two-hundred-foot slab avalanche, spewing snow dust that rose high overhead before crashing like a tidal wave, followed, slamming into the base facilities at perhaps two hundred miles per hour.

Five employees were in the patrol office on the second floor of the Summit Terminal Building. Two of them, Randy Buck and Tad DeFelice, stood in a part of the room protected by a twenty-two-foot boulder. The building's steel I-beam frame began to shake. Buck hit the floor, curling up for protection, as a wave of snow broke through the wall, engulfing him and pushing him violently across the floor. Fighting tightening bounds as the snow packed around him, he broke the surface and struggled to his feet. DeFelice was pinned alongside, standing in waist-deep snow. They were still in the room, but the foot-thick walls were gone. The other three employees, in parts of the room unprotected by the boulder, were blown out the back of the building. Buck, despite a broken rib and fracture of his vertebrae, began searching for the others. Two of the three, including manager Kingery, would be found dead. The third disappeared in the snow one hundred feet behind what remained of the building. Employees from the lodge saved him because he landed on his back, and one of his hands stuck out of the snow.

Two ski lifts were damaged beyond repair, as were several structures. Pieces of heavy equipment were mangled or crushed, having been carried hundreds of feet. Hundred-year-old trees had been snapped like twigs. The base lodge's windows were blown out, and tons of snow poured into the lounge and cafeteria on the second floor. The employees inside the lodge all survived. Three visitors from the Bay Area were not as lucky. Crossing the parking lot toward the building to see if there was food available, they were buried in ten to twelve feet of debris.

The slide had actually been three massive avalanches, starting atop different bowls some seven hundred feet above the resort. They had moved sympathetically and simultaneously. Larry Heywood, assistant patrol director at the time who went on to become an avalanche consultant for resorts throughout North America, described the avalanche as "a once in a century catastrophe . . . an event of geological time." As soon as the slide began to settle, employees probed and dug in buildings and the avalanche fields. After word went out, they were joined by volunteers and search-and-rescue personnel.

Employee Jake Smith had spent his last seconds transmitting the warning to others rather than trying to ride his snowmobile away from the wall of snow racing at him. He was wearing an avalanche rescue

Larry Heywood, later an avalanche consultant throughout North America, and Jim Plehn, who in the 1970s developed Alpine Meadows' state-of-the-art avalanche-control plan, gauge a slide's fault line. (Courtesy Jim Plehn)

transceiver that allowed him to be found as darkness was settling in. Six to eight volunteers dug frantically through the hardpack to get to him. Fifteen feet down, they found him standing upright, facing the avalanche. He had been buried for an hour and a half. Although as soon as they uncovered Jake's face a doctor performed mouth-to-mouth resuscitation, and patrollers began CPR before freeing him from the snow, the doctor soon pronounced him dead.

After the initial rescues, the discoveries were only of victims. Others were missing. But because snow had continued to fall and the danger of another avalanche threatened the lives of the rescuers, after the first day of searching the site had to be evacuated for three days.

Finally there was a break in the weather, and the searchers returned. Five days had passed since the avalanche when a miracle occurred. Anna Conrad, a twenty-two-year-old University of California–Davis graduate working as a lift operator, was found alive. She had been in the locker room of the Summit Terminal Building, down the hall from the patrol office, when the avalanche collapsed the mountain side wall. The impact knocked her down beneath a bench. The bank of lockers, falling over the bench, supported some fifteen feet of snow load and created a small airspace. She had subsisted on snow. She would lose her right leg below the knee and the toes from her left foot, but she survived 117 hours of being buried alive in the tiny space.

The snowfall for the ten days of storm totaled more than fourteen feet, nearly half the entire amount for an average season. The avalanche killed seven people and caused millions of dollars in damage.

The families of the three people killed crossing the parking lot filed a lawsuit, charging Alpine Meadows with negligence. Ski-industry executives throughout the country, in Europe, and around the world closely monitored the jury trial, held in 1985. It lasted five months with more than one hundred witnesses called. The primary expert for the plaintiffs had conducted terrain studies and analyzed data to conclude that potential run-out distances for an avalanche should have included the parking lot. He believed the twenty-year record kept by the ski area was not long enough to conclude that slopes that had not avalanched sympathetically might not. He contended that once people had been evacuated, signs or barricades should have been used to discourage reentry into the parking area. A second avalanche specialist testified in similar fashion.

An avalanche expert giving evidence for the defense observed that Alpine Meadows' avalanche record keeping was more complete than his own and that their interpretation of results was correct. A second defense authority concurred; he added that debris observed by patrollers below the slopes after the artillery discharges indicated stability. On the basis of the available information, he would have proceeded as had the defendants. A third defense expert explained that the criteria for hazard forecasts were meteorological conditions and historical performance patterns. He concluded that since storms as great or greater had struck the area previously without triggering a slide of such magnitude, this one could not have been foreseen.

The jury deliberated for two and a half weeks and appeared to be hung until the judge issued more specific instructions. He told the jurors to assess the actions of Alpine Meadows for standards of "ordinary care" with respect to the avalanche hazard in the parking lot. They then quickly found the resort nonnegligent: Before the event, highly trained professionals had made their best judgments and followed avalanche-control procedures. Although an appeal by the plaintiffs was settled out of court, the general conclusion drawn from the tragedy was that the avalanche was an unprecedented event, so its extraordinary results would have been nearly impossible to avert.

While the natural disaster derailed operations at Alpine Meadows, its neighboring resort, Squaw Valley, would suffer continuous difficulties, including ecological calamities and legal troubles, for many years running. Throughout the 1970s and 1980s, significant numbers of skiers stayed away from the resort. Owner Cushing was spending large amounts of time in the East, and the slopes, lifts, and facilities were not updated. The roof of the Olympic ice rink collapsed, and the facility had to be torn down. A 1986 *New York Times* story said skiers found the resort to have "ungroomed slopes, unappealing restaurants and uncooperative personnel."

In 1983 two thousand gallons of diesel fuel had spilled in the snow. Cushing paid a $350,000 fine after being found guilty of trying to hide the calamitous event. This was only the most egregious ecological offense, as yearly charges mounted against the resort for emitting pollutants into Squaw Creek. The water-quality board found the area's management to be repeat violators "who disputed almost every regulatory or enforcement action." To build a new tram, in 1989, Cushing ordered the cutting of more than eighteen hundred trees, many between three hundred and six hundred years old. The order violated terms of a conditional-use permit and a temporary superior court restraining order that was issued when the resort was threatened with litigation. The resort manager, who directed the cutting, later testified that Cushing urged the illegal action, saying, "What are they going to do, make us replant them?"

A neighbor, William R. Hewlett, the billionaire founder of Hewlett-Packard, joined by the Sierra Club and the Placer County district attorney, brought a suit against Cushing. Hewlett was an environmentalist with a history of trying to protect Lake Tahoe. In 1971 he bought land on Tahoe's shore and sold it to the Forest Service in order to prevent the construction of a massive condominium project. Now his action opposed Cushing for turning what had been a "cathedral-like canyon" into "Tram Basin Bowl." The legal action was dubbed in the press "Silicon Valley versus Squaw Valley."

The court found for Hewlett, imposing $223,000 in penalties on Cushing; ordered a permanent injunction against further development of land where the clear-cutting occurred; and issued an order to return the area to its natural state. It also awarded attorney fees to Hewlett and the Sierra Club that amounted to some $1 million. On appeal the California Court of Appeals upheld the lower court's finding. It called Squaw Valley's attitude disdainful and cavalier, commenting that the record "is replete with evidence of Squaw Valley's complete disregard for procedures designed to protect the environment and forest resources." Regarding the clear-cut trees, it concluded, "Squaw Valley's actions destroyed an irreplaceable natural treasure."

For ten years, during and after the litigation, Squaw Valley continued missing compliance deadlines for water quality while averaging more than one violation of standards a year. Finally, in 2000, the federal Environmental Protection Agency became involved. It undertook a two-year probe of whether the resort had contravened the Clean Water Act before concluding that it lacked evidence against the ski area. The problems Cusing faced with regulators were mainly the result of his pushing ahead plans that would improve accessibility and amenities at the resort: new runs, high-speed quad chairlifts, and a $15 million renovation at the top terminal of the aerial cable car. The renovation included restaurants, tennis courts, a swimming lagoon, and a new ice rink.

When Cushing died in 2006, his third wife, Nancy Wendt Cushing, an attorney who had worked alongside him during the resort's transformation, succeeded him as president. Wendt Cushing brought a perspective of environmental stewardship to Squaw Valley. She established an entire department dedicated to vegetation and environmental management, making the resort one of the first in the world to do so. Squaw Valley now spent between $200,000 and $1 million a year on conservation and, touted as "the Comeback Kid," has been consistently rated among the top ski areas in the country for its environmental efforts.

Changes in the environment have changed the behaviors of some Tahoe wildlife, notably *Ursus americanus californiensis,* the black bear, often cinnamon or brown in color. Several hundred are estimated to live in the basin. Black bears grow larger in northern latitudes than in southern, and those in the Sierra are among the largest in the country, including six- and seven-hundred-pounders. They are not often aggressive, and, although humans have been mauled to death in other states, no human has ever been killed by a black bear in California or Nevada. Nevertheless, with the great influx of humans, the bears became worrisome. Unless hibernating, black bears are nearly always hungry, and once they find a place to acquire food, they return to it. Dog food, bird feed, and garbage are especially enticing. Food inside unoccupied houses is also tempting, since bears learn to open doors and refrigerators and break into pantries.

In September 1998 a renter in Homewood stored garbage at a cabin, and a neighbor was frightened by a bear attempting to get it. The renter contacted the California Department of Fish and Game. Following department policy, the agency issued a depredation permit, which allowed the bear to be killed. The renter then hired one of the department's contract trappers, who trapped and killed the wrong bear and one of her cubs. A second cub had to be rescued from the top of a tree. Within weeks, three women, Kathy Travernier and Linda Brown, two local teachers, and Ann Bryant, who was doing wildlife rehabilitation work, organized the Bear League. They set a goal of avoiding any more unnecessary killing. Fish and Game, at first leery, later took to the idea of having community members respond to complaints. Bryant became the league's executive director; Travernier and Brown served on the organization's board. The Bear League arranged seminars to educate the public in methods of averting problems associated with living in bear country. Volunteers learned to field calls and respond to all kinds of emergencies involving bears.

The Bear League experienced success, gaining nine hundred members by 2005 and disseminating information to thousands of residents and visitors. Still, there were setbacks. One of the most publicized occurred in February 2005, when a couple from the Sierra foothills visited their cabin on Tahoe's west shore to find approximately $100,000 of damage. Bears had gained entrance through an unsecured door. Called by the Placer County sheriff's deputies, director Bryant said she had never seen bears inflict worse damage in a Tahoe house. She discovered a small sow hibernating in a crawl space beneath the cabin. Bryant wanted to scare the bear out of the space and board up the area so it could not return. The cabin owners decided to just let the bear continue to hibernate there, securing the trapdoor so it could not get back into the house. But the insurance company refused to inspect the damaged structure until the bear was removed.

The owners then contacted Fish and Game, obtained a permit, and hired three men from the Central Valley to shoot the bear. When the contract trappers entered the space, there were three bears: two cubs had been sleeping behind the mother. The contractors claimed that the animals attacked, and they had to kill all three in self-defense. Although Bryant wanted the contractors put on trial to prove their claim, the deputy district attorney commented, "Who are we to say [the attack] didn't happen. My gut feeling is it probably didn't, but I doubt criminal charges can be filed."

The contractors became enraged when, rather than allowing them to dispose of the dead bears, the game warden decided to do it; claws and gall bladders can be worth as much as $20,000. With the incident reported in the media as far away as San Francisco, the cabin owners received dozens of angry calls. Once the cabin was repaired, vandals damaged it again, breaking windows and smashing things inside. Wires and gas lines cut on the snow blower confirmed that humans had done the damage. The publicity caused the cabin owners such misery that they sold their cabin and left the area. Word of the tragedy had the opposite effect for bears, raising sympathy. By the end of the year, the Bear League's membership had increased to fourteen hundred.

Ann Bryant and the Bear League have joined California Indian tribes in lobbying the legislature to reduce bear hunting. League members have joined with Washoe Indian elders and children, the Forest Service, and local nurseries to plant berry bushes far up in the mountains in attempts to keep the bears away from neighborhoods. Bryant once took forty inner-city teenagers into the mountains to build dens for bears to hibernate in to keep them out from under homes. At the conclusion of the workday, with the young people sitting exhausted above a small pond, a 250-pound bear came from the underbrush to swim not more than thirty or forty feet from them. Coming out of the water, it shook off, spraying droplets that Bryant described as creating "a rainbow in the sunlight," and ambled back into the bushes, a fitting ending to the experience for the city teens. By 2010 the Bear League had nearly fifteen hundred members throughout the United States, with two hundred trained volunteers so that the league might respond quickly in any neighborhood in the Tahoe Basin where there is an incident involving a bear.

As with other animals, many times when a bear cub is found orphaned, it is taken to Tom and Cheryl Milham, founders of Lake Tahoe Wildlife Care on the south shore. Theirs is the only care facility licensed by the State of California to rehabilitate cubs. Beginning in 1978 they opened their home to injured small animals and birds. For more than thirty years they have operated the nationally recognized center that serves injured or orphaned wild birds and animals at Tahoe as well as nine surrounding counties. The Milhams' facility contains cages specially built for bears, coyotes, or raccoons; an aviary; a mew for eagles, hawks, or owls; and special tanks for river otters. Once a year the center hosts an open house; the rest of the year it is all business. There are no tours and no visitors allowed, as the Milhams and their volunteers raise and assist the animals to mend in order to release them back into the wilderness.

In 2009 the center cared for 726 birds and animals. Of these, although 291 expired or needed to be euthanized, 435 were successfully released or transferred for permanent care. All species are accepted, from a 97-pound mountain lion found running loose in the Tahoe Keys; to baby cliff swallows, who needed to be fed every fifteen minutes, fourteen hours a day; to Lil' Smokey, a three-month-old, six-pound bear cub with burned paws from a forest fire. Lil' Smokey brought widespread attention to the facility as ten television stations videotaped one of the every-other-day dressing changes on his paws.

In 2009 the center housed three bald eagles. One, a fledgling too weak to perch or fly, spent weeks lying down or sitting in the merganser cage. When the bird gained enough strength, the Milhams moved it to the mew, and after it spent several months feasting on fish donated by local fishermen, they took it out to try its wings. The first couple of trials it could not fly thirty feet. They placed it on a weighted line tied to its ankle, and it exercised and strengthened its wings. Tom Milham once remarked on eagles and their kin, "Most raptors, when you look in their eyes, they give you the feeling they are in charge." When this young eagle gained full strength, Milham, accompanied by a group of volunteers,

Too weak to perch, a young eagle feasted on fish and trained at Lake Tahoe Wildlife Care before being released back into the wild. (Courtesy Lake Tahoe Wildlife Care Center)

released it from high on a hill. It caught a thermal and circled before them. "Finally, he was soaring away from us," said Milham, "still circling . . . until he was no longer in sight. Our hearts were in our throats. We felt very confident about his chances in the wild."

Until the end of the twentieth century, the only sitting U.S. president ever to visit Lake Tahoe was Rutherford B. Hayes, who passed through in 1880. That changed in 1997 when President Bill Clinton brought an important contingent of executive-branch officials to the lake. He came not to visit but to focus the nation's attention on the lake as a national resource and develop policies to protect it. Besides Clinton and Vice President Al Gore, the secretary of agriculture, the secretary of the interior, and the executive director of the Environmental Protection Agency attended, as did California's and Nevada's governors and U.S. senators, local government officials, and leaders of the lake's interest groups. The summit featured workshops and negotiations that one local businessman described as creating policy in "a bottom-up process, and not top-down." Despite Clinton's strict ongoing efforts to balance the federal budget by cutting spending, he pledged $24 million a year for two years to finance twenty-seven proposals to improve the lake's environment.

Rochelle Nason, the executive director of the League to Save Lake Tahoe, was one of the organizers of the summit. "It was very exciting

Rochelle Nason, executive director of the League to Save Lake Tahoe, presents a photograph to Vice President Al Gore at the 1997 Lake Tahoe Presidential Summit. (Courtesy the League to Save Lake Tahoe)

and very heartening that people came together like they did," she observed. "It [built] relationships among environmental, business and property rights groups. It was a galvanizing event." Nason, who had directed the league since 1993, had echoed the sentiment of Vice President Gore, who spoke of one of the surprising findings during the national leaders' visit: "We intend to celebrate the unique partnerships that have occurred in all parts of the Tahoe Basin community. Many other places in the country don't have this kind of cooperation. But in this special place, the business community and the environmentalists have resolved their conflicts and come together with one voice."

The tangible result of the summit was the appropriation by Congress of $424 million for restoration projects. The perception of everyone's agreeing on the means of achieving the same goals did not last. By 2009 Nason and the league were again battling the TRPA. The argument was reminiscent of those in the 1980s or even the 1950s. Nason stressed preserving the qualities of the lake for future generations by allowing growth only within the bounds of the established scientific threshold standards. The bistate agency sought to find new funding for environmental rehabilitation by enlisting business partners in redevelopments.

Fighting the region's bleak financial outlook, with Tahoe gaming apparently in permanent decline, TRPA officials hoped "smart growth" would allow it to again thrive economically while making environmental improvements to commercial core areas. The TRPA's new direction, focusing on the urban areas that encompass 15 percent of the landmass but produce 72 percent of the lake's pollution, encouraged reinvestment, bringing old buildings up to new standards. The TRPA proposed to allow taller buildings with higher population density to replace old structures. In return, the agency would require new construction to result in environment-enhancing structures with the latest storm-water and erosion controls.

The league was adamant in its objections. "'Smart growth' is an excellent strategy for urbanized areas, where growth is inevitable," commented Nason. "But it is not smart to apply it to Tahoe, a sensitive area that is threatened by growth and overuse." The league supported natural-resources tourism and density changes that would reduce traffic in Tahoe. And so the old battle was rejoined: During the previous fifteen years, the league had filed one lawsuit; now, within a matter of months, it filed three.

At the same time, Lake Tahoe's demographics have changed dramatically. At the turn of the twenty-first century some 36 percent of California residents statewide and 22 percent of Nevadans were of Hispanic origin, and large numbers of Mexican American, South American, and Mexican immigrants had moved to the lake. Estimates were that Hispanics made up more than 25 percent of the fifty-five thousand total Tahoe Basin residents. The political achievements of Norma Santiago, born in Puerto Rico, were emblematic of the population shift. She served as a board member on the TRPA and was elected as the Lake Tahoe representative to the El Dorado County Board of Supervisors in a special election in 2005. A resident of the lake since 1982, the University of California–Berkeley graduate had a broad constituency. Along with other civic service, she served for years as a board member for the Tahoe Women's Center. That her popularity ran across ethnic lines was demonstrated in the general election of 2006, when her reelection campaign for the county board netted her an overwhelming 78.5 percent of the vote.

At the time of the Tahoe Presidential Summit Charles Goldman, who had become known as the lake's "father" of ecological research, was nearing the end of his long tenure as the lake's primary scientific expert. Clinton and Gore took time to ride along with him on a water-monitoring cruise. Although Goldman praised the two leaders' quick grasp of marine science, his ability to teach certainly factored into their acuity. After all, Goldman's ability to present data in ways that laypeople could understand served as the impetus for the "save the lake" movement. In 1969 when members of the Water Quality Control Board wrote, "It can be conclusively stated that the clarity of Lake Tahoe has not decreased since the lake was first sampled in 1873," it was Goldman who proved them wrong. Using aerial photographs, he displayed how sediments and nutrients were causing "spectacular local increases in turbidity." The programs of pumping sewage effluent out of the basin were instituted because Goldman convinced officials that even treated sewage would seriously degrade the water quality of the lake. And his findings were instrumental in developing erosion-control measures and vegetation-protection guidelines. It was Goldman who explained how algae in the lake had changed, feeding on phosphorus rather than the nitrogen of earlier years. This led to the conclusion that streamborne phosphorus and trace metals needed to be reduced by limiting soil disturbances and restoring wetlands.

Goldman helped found the Tahoe Research Group at Sierra Nevada College in Incline Village. It is housed in a state-of-the-art research facility, one of only five science laboratories in the world to receive the U.S. Green Building Council's highest award, Platinum LEED Certification. The facility hosts scientists from TERC (the University of California–Davis's Tahoe Research Group), the University of Nevada, the U.S. Forest Service, the U.S. Geological Survey, and the Desert Research Institute. The research group encourages multidisciplinary work meant to provide scientific information for restoration and sustainable use of Lake Tahoe and its environs.

By 2005 Goldman could conclude, "With all the work that's going on in the Basin, we feel we're beginning to win the battle against declining clarity in Lake Tahoe." Unfortunately, a serious setback two years later brought his findings on phosphorous and nitrogen to the fore along the Upper Truckee River. On a windy Sunday afternoon in late June 2007, several 911 calls reported smoke in Meyers, off Upper Truckee Road. Dispatchers told the callers there was a prescribed burn in the area and did not immediately alert the nearby fire stations. The Tahoe area had been suffering through several years of drought, and the snowpack that year had been only 29 percent of normal. The smoke turned out to be other than the dispatchers believed. In an area commonly used by partygoers, failure to extinguish an illegal campfire had allowed it to escape.

The fire raged for a week, carried toward the lake by fierce winds. A total of 186 engines and 21 helicopters were deployed along with 2,180 firefighters—some from as far away as San Bernardino, California. At one point the flames changed direction without warning, and firefighters were forced to deploy their individual fire shelters, pulling the aluminized tents over themselves for protection. As ash fell from the sky, mass evacuations took place in neighborhoods in the fire's potential paths. In the end, the blaze consumed 3,072 acres of forest, destroyed 254 homes, and displaced more than 1,000 people. Stands of majestic cedars, rare mosses, and northern goshawk territory had been annihilated. Brook trout were found belly-up in the river.

Along with the loss of wildlife habitat were the tragic losses suffered by humans and the $160 million loss of property. Goldman offered a bleak assessment for the long-term effects on the lake. The fire had burned 5 percent to 10 percent of the Upper Truckee watershed. The phosphorous and nitrogen from the ash would typically recycle through the lake for five to twenty years. Goldman warned, "Fire sediments settle so slowly they will impact [the lake's] transparency for a longer period of time."

Still, the worst effects of the fire were mitigated. Federal, state, and local governments combined resources to immediately remove structural debris and implement erosion-control measures. After two weeks there had been no measurable change in the clarity of the lake. Throughout the summer and fall, planes were used to seed and mulch the burn area, while features were installed to revitalize streams and control runoff. Near-term measures were completed by October 2007, and review and maintenance procedures were formulated to be implemented over the following ten years.

The ongoing battle to preserve the lake's health reflects its value to those who visit as well as those who have made homes there. At the Tahoe Presidential Summit, Vice President Gore repeated a theme famously introduced by Thomas Starr King. Gore observed that Tahoe's significance to the nation goes beyond its popularity as a recreational destination: "Natural beauty like Lake Tahoe's concentrates the soul and leads to a deeper appreciation for the beauty of life." Through their work the many visual artists who live at the lake give credence to this idea. Among them are photographer Jim Hildinger of Angora Lake, South Shore painters Peter Darvis and Thomas Easley, and bronze sculptor David Foster. Truckee artist Cathee Van Rossem-St. Clair is unique in illustrating the fragility of life by eschewing canvases for eggshells, paint-

Artist Dan Jones's children's memorial, midtown South Tahoe. Note the broken strap on the log, symbolizing the children's spirits lifting it. (Courtesy Dan Jones)

ing intricate scenes on shells as large as that of an ostrich or as small as that of a quail.

The artist perhaps most associated with Tahoe is Dan Jones, a painter and sculptor who has lived on the south shore more than forty years. It is his twenty-five-foot faux-granite welcome sign in the shape of the lake that has greeted visitors entering South Lake Tahoe on Highway 50 since 1995. Midway through town, Jones also created a memorial out of a tree trunk attached with straps to a sculpted boulder. The trunk has nameplates affixed to honor local children who have lost their lives. One of the straps is broken, as if demonstrating the power of the children's spirits rising. Jones has created installations, utilizing painted mural backgrounds and artificial rocks and trees combined with real waterfalls and ponds, to bring the forest inside homes around the lake. A prime example of his skill in sculpting and painting cement that becomes indistinguishable from granite is the four-foot wall, waterfall, and baptismal font inside St. Francis of Assisi Catholic Church at Incline Village.

Performance artist McAvoy Layne, who lives at Incline Village, is also inexorably linked to the lake. A Mark Twain impersonator, Layne has entertained audiences at Russia's Leningrad University and on stages in Europe and across the United States. He has been featured on television specials and performed in Tahoe venues from casinos to daily stints on the lake's four-hundred-passenger paddle wheeler. Layne's presentations are distinguished by his quick wit and Twain scholarship, he has presented a paper at several Quadrennial Scholars' Conferences at the Center for Mark Twain Studies in Elmira, New York.

In 2009 retired Forest Service hydrologist Larry Schmidt, searching to determine the route of a pioneer trail, discovered the east-shore cove where Mark Twain camped in 1861. Although contested by another researcher, historian Robert Stewart's fact-finding on the site led to a proposal to the Nevada State Board on Geographic Names that the site be named Clemens Cove. In his unique style, McAvoy Layne gave justification for affixing Twain's name to the feature: "Kit Carson, who passed through this area as quickly as he could, has a mountain range, a city, a valley, a river, a sink, and a summit named for him. Yes and Mark Twain, who glorified the lake in his writing, has only one little town out on Highway 50 with a bar and two motorcycles sitting in front. Let's name the cove for Twain." In September 2010 the Nevada Board submitted the name "Sam Clemens Cove" for approval by the U.S. secretary of the interior.

In 1999 Bob Kingman, a Tahoe native, worked for the Tahoe Conservancy developing sustainable recreation. He was researching bike trails, but at a trails conference he happened on a session discussing

McAvoy Layne pursuing a Mark Twain pastime on the "faro table" at Clemens Cove. (Courtesy Robert Stewart)

water trails, or blueways. These trails, in which nonmotorized craft follow marked or mapped waterways, were practically unknown at the time. There were perhaps two or three water trails in all California. The more Kingman thought about it, the more perfect the concept seemed for Tahoe. It utilized a low-impact, potentially revenue-generating form of recreation. If visitors circumnavigated the lake, they would be in the basin multiple days, camping or renting motel rooms, seeing the lake from a new perspective. They would be out of their cars, thereby limiting air pollution, and would help the economy as they used resources along the shore.

Trying out the trail one early morning, as Kingman floated twenty-five yards off the east shore, he noticed an animal cutting through the surface of the placid water. The small creature dove and, a minute later, popped up with a crayfish in its claws. It was a mink, the most aquatic of the weasel family, and as Kingman watched from a few feet away, it climbed onto a rock, groomed itself, and feasted on its shellfish breakfast. Kingman had seen firsthand the unique quality of the water trail. Those moving quietly along it might catch sight of the otters, beavers, ospreys, bald eagles, or mergansers not readily seen by those off the water or in motorized boats.

In 2003 a group of civic leaders, called Tahoe Tomorrow, who worked to broaden the image of Tahoe, heard of his idea and enlisted Kingman to implement the concept. An all-volunteer committee met regularly for a year, developing a water-trail map. The guide provided all the information needed to use the water trail, including campgrounds and other lodging, eateries, public boat launches and parking, emergency contacts, public beaches, flora, and fauna. The printing of the waterproof maps was funded by several groups, including the TRPA, civic organizations, chambers of commerce, and the Nevada Division of Wildlife. The sponsorship alliance illustrated the nearly universal acceptance of this type of recreational activity at the lake.

Another low-impact recreational activity was the brainchild of Glenn Hampton, a tall man with a long stride. When he lived at Tahoe people had difficulty keeping up with him when hiking or when he wished to push through a project. Coming to the lake as the recreation and resource officer for the Forest Service in 1977, he observed that the area with the most developed trail system, the Desolation Wilderness on the southwest side of the lake, was being overused. The Dardanelles area, in the southeast, also had ample trails and steady use, but there were almost no trails, and little employment of lands, above the north and east shores. Hampton decided it would help diffuse use if a continuous trail, with feeder trails throughout the network, followed the rim of the lake's surrounding mountains.

He studied the old Washoe trails and those of the early pioneers and the Basque sheepherders. Once he developed a general plan, he began recruiting volunteers who would design, build, and maintain the trail. Between 1984, when the building began atop Luther Pass, and 2001, when the last section between Rose Knob Peak and Mount Baldy was completed, some ten thousand people worked on the Tahoe Rim Trail. The 165-mile route hosts equestrians, hikers, runners, and, outside the wilderness areas, mountain bikers. Parts of it afford wheelchair access. It ranges in elevation from 6,300 to 10,300 feet, traversing deep forests of old-growth hemlock, red fir, and Jeffrey pine; meadows with chest-high wildflowers; pristine lakes; and towering granite peaks. Offering views of the lake throughout, it is one of the most beautiful hiking trails in the country.

David Antonucci, a local historian who worked many years as an environmental engineer at the lake, found an overgrown trail while walking in Ed Z'berg Sugar Pine Point State Park in Tahoma. The trail had been lost over time; even the park rangers did not know its history. Investigating, Antonucci discovered it was part of one of the 1960 Olympic cross-country ski and biathalon courses, constructed along the west shore. Considered to be the first cross-country ski area in the nation, the Nordic trails are rolling single-lane paths. Not satisfied with having discovered the site, Antonucci organized a group to locate and map the course's features. Now fourteen miles of the Nordic trails have been restored. The California Parks Department, inspired by Antonucci's group, has erected interpretive signs that tell of the 1960 Olympics and the race courses at Tahoma. The trails are groomed in snow season and open for hiking and cycling in summer, providing miles of quiet passage through a majestic pine forest replete with Olympic lore.

Whether experienced from the water trail, the rim trail, an Olympic course, or any locale, Lake Tahoe's waters and surrounding mountains exhibit a timeless quality. The marring of the landscape by clear-cutting its forests and incessant development remains evident, although not as pervasive as in other eras. Filled-in marshes and algae in the lake continue to require rehabilitation. In some areas, cluttered buildings line the roadways, oversized gambling palaces crowd Stateline, and developments of interminable condominiums can be found lakeside and mountainside. Still, ongoing scientific studies now make it less likely that environmental standards can be shunted aside in favor of economic interests. Since the Presidential Summit in 1997, what is now referred to as the "Tahoe Summit" has been held annually, focusing government attention on the lake and creating an opportunity for national, state, and local officials to seek remedies to the area's problems.

Moreover, Tahoe's ecosystems, while continuing to require particular care, have proved surprisingly resilient. Depleted forests have grown back. Water clarity has stabilized and, owing to regulations reducing pollutants has shown modest improvement: a gain of eight feet over the past twenty years.

Although the individuals have changed, from Native people who protected it, to American residents and businesspeople, to those who would nurse the area back to health, it is the same lake and the same setting. Tahoe can be awe-inspiring viewed at dawn or twilight, during a summer squall, or in the silence of a snowstorm.

For many hundreds of years, continuing to the present day, Washoes have regarded the lake as the center of their world. Others who came later have realized its significance; some have found it to provide spiritual solace. Poets continue to remark on it, scientists to evaluate data and provide strategies to revitalize it. Withal, the lake survives as the jewel of the Sierra, one of America's special places.

Selected Bibliography

Antonucci, David C. *Snowball's Chance: The Story of the 1960 Olympic Winter Games, Squaw Valley, and Lake Tahoe.* Charleston, S.C.: BookSurge Publishing, 2009.

Brewer, William Henry. *Up and Down California in 1860–1864: The Journal of William H. Brewer.* New Haven: Yale University Press, 1930.

Browne, J. Ross. *A Peep at Washoe and Washoe Revisited.* Balboa Island, Calif.: Paisano Press, 1959.

Frohlich, Robert. *Mountain Dreamers: Visionaries of Sierra Nevada Skiing.* Truckee, Calif.: Coldstream Press, 1997.

Glasscock, C. B. *Lucky Baldwin: The Story of an Unconventional Success.* Reno: Silver Syndicate Press, 1993.

Goin, Peter. *Then and Now: South Lake Tahoe.* Charleston, S.C.: Arcadia Press, 2010.

Hauserman, Tim. *The Tahoe Rim Trail: A Complete Guide for Hikers, Mountain Bikers, and Equestrians.* Berkeley: Wilderness Press, 2002.

Hinkle, George, and Bliss Hinkle. *Sierra-Nevada Lakes.* Reno: University of Nevada Press, 1987.

Howard, Thomas Frederick. *Sierra Crossing: First Roads to California.* Berkeley and Los Angeles: University of California Press, 1998.

James, George Wharton. *The Lake of the Sky: Lake Tahoe.* Chicago: Charles T. Powner, 1956.

James, Ronald M. *The Roar and the Silence: A History of Virginia City and the Comstock Lode.* Reno: University of Nevada Press, 1998.

James, Ronald M., and Susan A. James. *Castle in the Sky: George Whittell Jr. and the Thunderbird Lodge.* Lake Tahoe: Thunderbird Lodge Preservation Society, 2002.

Laxalt, Robert. *Nevada: A Bicentennial History.* 1977. Reprint, Reno: University of Nevada Press, 1991.

Layne, McAvoy. *Becoming Mark Twain*. Incline Village, Nev.: Trends Publishing, 2009.

Makley, Matthew S., and Michael J. Makley. *Cave Rock: Climbers, Courts, and a Washoe Indian Sacred Site*. Reno: University of Nevada Press, 2010.

Meschery, Joanne. *Truckee: An Illustrated History of the Town and Its Surroundings*. Truckee, Calif.: Rocking Stone Press, 1978.

Nevers, Jo Ann. *Wa She Shu: A Washo Tribal History*. Reno: Inter-Tribal Council of Nevada, 1976.

Obermayr, Erich. *Foot Path to Four-Lane: A Historical Guidebook to Transportation on Lake Tahoe's Southeast Shore*. Carson City: State of Nevada Department of Transportation, 2005.

Orsi, Richard J. *Sunset Limited: The Southern Pacific Railroad and the Development of the West*. Berkeley and Los Angeles: University of California Press, 2005.

Scott, Edward B. *The Saga of Lake Tahoe*. Vol. 1. Crystal Bay, Nev.: Sierra-Tahoe Publishing, 1957.

———. *The Saga of Lake Tahoe*. Vol. 2. Crystal Bay, Nev.: Sierra-Tahoe Publishing, 1973.

Strong, Douglas H. *Tahoe: From Timber Barons to Ecologists*. Lincoln: University of Nebraska Press, 1999.

Twain, Mark. *Roughing It*. Hartford, Conn.: Hartford Press, 1899.

Wheeler, Sessions S., with William W. Bliss. *Tahoe Heritage: The Bliss Family of Glenbrook, Nevada*. Reno: University of Nevada Press, 1992.

Woodlief, Jennifer. *A Wall of White: The True Story of Heroism and Survival in the Face of a Deadly Avalanche*. New York: Atria Books, 2009.

Index